Devotions
for
Clutterers

Devotions for Clutterers

MELODY CARLSON

CROSSAMERICA BOOKS

CROSSINGS BOOK CLUB, GARDEN CITY, NEW YORK

© 2004 by Melody Carlson
All rights reserved.

CrossAmerica Books is an imprint and trademark
pending on behalf of Crossings Book Club.

Scripture quotations used in this book are from the New Revised
Standard Version Bible, copyright © 1989 by the Division of
Christian Education of the National Council of the Churches of
Christ in the USA, used by permission, all rights reserved.

Cover design by Sherry Sumerlin
Interior design by Debbie Glasserman

ISBN: 0-7394-4100-0

Printed in the United States of America

Devotions
for
Clutterers

Oh, to Be Clutter Free

He reached from on high, he took me,
he drew me out of mighty waters.

—2 Samuel 22:17

Don't we all long for order in our lives? Don't we dream of a home that is an uncluttered place of peace, a calm haven, a comfortable refuge? Perhaps we don't even realize how we may be sabotaging that dream by unwittingly *inviting* disorder into our lives. Maybe we've grown oblivious to how nonessentials heap themselves on us until we can barely navigate our way through the piles. Yet even as we drown in a sea of clutter, we desperately search the horizon for a tranquil island where order reigns. But how can we get there?

First we must recognize that our cluttering habits are stressful—that they deplete our energies and steal our serenity. And we must choose to change them. But our clutter won't just disappear. No, junk mail will keep pouring in, laundry will pile high, *stuff* will accumulate—if we let it. But let's not give up. Instead, let's take the first step on a long journey. And with a conscious effort and God's help, we *can* choose to lead a more orderly life.

FOR FURTHER REFLECTION

1. *Are you fed up with clutter?*
2. *Does it feel as if things rule you instead of you ruling them?*
3. *Are you ready to change your life?*

PRAYER

Dear God, I want to be free from my cluttering habits.
I long for order in my life. Please help me. Amen

When Enough Is Enough

. . . and my people shall be satisfied
with my bounty, says the Lord.

—Jeremiah 31:14

Our culture tends to be led by consumerism. So, is it any wonder we're surrounded by too much of everything? We are constantly bombarded with promises that new products will make our lives complete. But when will we ever have enough? Perhaps the problem isn't that we don't have everything we need, but that we never seem to be satisfied with all we have. Do we honestly believe that something else, something new, something different . . . will fulfill that craving within us—that place that always yearns for something more?

Perhaps what we really long for can only come from God. Maybe what we desire is His touch upon our lives—His grace, His peace, His goodness. Perhaps if we allow ourselves to experience what God has to offer, we will also experience a real and lasting satisfaction. And then we'll learn to live much more happily without all the unnecessary clutter in our lives.

FOR FURTHER REFLECTION

1. *Are you a victim of consumer-targeted advertising?*
2. *Do you purchase items you don't really need or want?*
3. *Do you think material things will make you happy?*
4. *What would happen if you made a commitment to refrain from making impulsive purchases?*

PRAYER

Lord, teach me to seek my contentment from You.
Show me that only You can satisfy my deepest longings. Amen

Clutter Is in the Eye of the Beholder

Do not be conformed to this world,
but be transformed by the renewing of your minds,
so that you may discern what is the will of God—
what is good and acceptable and perfect.
—Romans 12:2

To get a handle on clutter, we need to understand it more fully. Which means we must actually look around and *see* it—it's amazing how many clutterers have become adept at *not* seeing their clutter! You might try taking some photographs of your living space; sometimes a photo sheds new light on a situation. (And just think of the before and after shots you'll have later on!) Once our eyes are opened to clutter problems, we begin to realize that it's all around us.

The temptation might be to overreact—to just throw it all away. But this is simply going from one extreme to the other, and something we might ultimately regret. After all, one man's trash can truly be another man's treasure (just toss out your husband's favorite old golf shoes and you'll see). There are some general ways to determine what is clutter and what isn't, but just remember clutter differs for all, so develop a discerning eye.

IS IT CLUTTER OR NOT?

Ask yourself the following as you begin to sort through your clutter. If you answer yes to any of these questions, the item probably should not be thrown away:
1. *Does anyone use this?*
2. *Do I enjoy having this in my life?*
3. *Does this have sentimental value?*
4. *I've got more than one of these—do I really need them all?*

PRAYER

God, help me to become more discerning about all things.
And specifically help me to determine
what is and is not clutter. Amen

A Place for Everything . . .

You will decide on a matter, and it will be established
for you, and light will shine on your ways.

—Job 22:28

We've heard it for years. We've probably said it ourselves. But do we live it? Do we really have a place for *everything*? And do we keep everything in its place? Probably not. So let's explore this old adage a little further. A place for everything suggests that if we own something, we should have a place to keep it. Therefore, if we don't have a place for a certain item, perhaps we shouldn't own that item. Or, maybe the item taking its place needs to go. Somehow we must balance our objects and space.

And to do this, we must change habits. First we must be willing to admit our space is limited. Next we must discipline ourselves to put things away—where they belong—before they take root in the wrong place! This will take time and commitment. But once this *putting things away* habit is established our lives will become much more manageable.

SPACE VS. STUFF

1. *How much space do you really have?*
2. *Is your space being used the way you'd like it to be?*
3. *Your amount of space should determine your amount of stuff; begin to thin out the stuff.*

PRAYER

Heavenly Father, You created a beautiful world.
Teach me to create a beautiful atmosphere
in my home. Amen

A Matter of Trust

Trust in the Lord with all your heart,
and do not rely on your own insight.

—Proverbs 3:5

Okay, so we've begun to think about the clutter in our lives, and perhaps we've even taken our first steps toward controlling it. But what keeps us from marching forward and ruthlessly clearing out years' worth of accumulated stuff? What stops us from getting rid of the unnecessary?

Could it be a simple matter of trust? Have we mistakenly come to believe that God's ability to give and to bless is limited to the stuff within our homes? Do we fear that if we give something away today, we will suddenly be miserable without it tomorrow? Has our affinity for clutter undermined our ability to trust God? Maybe it's time to ask ourselves a few challenging questions.

YOUR TRUST QUOTIENT

1. *Can you trust God to take care of you?*
2. *Can you trust that God will provide all you need?*
3. *Can you trust that God wants a better life for you?*
4. *Can you trust that God will lead you?*

PRAYER

Gracious God, I confess I have trouble trusting You
sometimes. Help me to trust that You will provide
and care for me. Amen

Facing the Clutter Monster Within

Take no part in the unfruitful works
of darkness, but instead expose them.
—Ephesians 5:11

Have you ever felt like you're being held captive by a cruel and evil clutter monster? You look around your house and it seems hopeless. It's like a living, breathing beast has taken your home hostage and will never let it go. But did you know that the clutter monster is you? And just as you are the one who allowed these problems to pile up, you are the only one who can make them go away. But it takes discipline and determination.

Let's start small. We need to realize that like any other demon, clutter monsters *love* the darkness. They don't like to be exposed. So, look around your home and work spaces. Are there any areas that are shadowy or poorly lit? Does the lack of good lighting offer a place for the clutter monster to hide his treasures? Remember that it's easier to ignore clutter when you can't see it.

LIGHTEN UP

1. *Look for the dark corners in your home, and find ways to lighten them up.*
2. *Check the wattage of your light bulbs. Can you safely upgrade?*
3. *Would a new clip-on light help illuminate what's hiding on your desk?*
4. *Consider under-the-counter light strips or spots for your kitchen.*

PRAYER

Dear Lord, help me to recognize the clutter monster is me,
and help me to change. Shine Your light and show me the way.
Amen

The Battle Against Stuff

Take action, for it is your duty,
and we are with you; be strong, and do it.

—Ezra 10:4

Stuff happens. Every day more of it enters our lives. The mailman delivers it, our children dump it on the floor, our spouses drop it on the countertop. So, how do we cope with this steady barrage of stuff? First of all, we should recognize that we can't stop all of it from coming, but we *can* stop it from collecting.

We can do this by dealing with stuff as soon as it hits us. We don't give it a chance to pile up. We toss out our junk mail while we sort through the rest. We create and use a filing system for any other paper items that we need to keep (bills, records, correspondence). We help our children establish their own places to keep their things. We create places to collect items to be given away. And we discipline ourselves to throw things out.

PAPER TRAIL

1. *Make a paper recycling center out of a crate or tub and use it.*
2. *Create an easy-to-use file system—organize it any way you like. If space is limited, you might drape a two-drawer file cabinet with a tablecloth and use it as an end table.*
3. *Place a "transition" basket or box near the doorway for papers that are coming and going (bills, permission slips, letters to be mailed, etc.). Check it daily.*

PRAYER

God, help me to see the importance of being vigilant
in my battle against the clutter and accumulation in my life.
Amen

Chaos Central

Our steps are made firm by the Lord,
when he delights in our way.

—Psalm 37:23

It's morning again. Time for children to get ready for school, time for others to get ready for work. And that's when the chaos usually begins: "I can't find any brown socks." "Where's my book report on Egypt?" "How come all these cereal boxes are empty?" "Did my soccer jersey ever get washed?"

Welcome to Chaos Central. We've all been here from time to time; some of us have taken up permanent residence. But a little planning, a little order can change all that. We may need to do some preorganizing the night before, or rise twenty minutes earlier. But the more streamlined and clutter free we become, the better our chances of escaping Chaos Central.

PLANNING AHEAD

1. *Make use of your "transition" basket to place items needed for the next day.*
2. *Attach a "shopping list" tablet to your refrigerator for people to list needed items.*
3. *Delegate responsibility so everyone doesn't come to you for everything. (For example, you can teach older children how to do their own laundry.)*

PRAYER

Loving Father, I know You are a God of peace, not chaos.
Help me to learn new ways to establish calm
and order in my mornings. Amen

Hang On, I'm Still Looking

So let us not grow weary in doing what is right,
for we will reap at harvest time, if we do not give up.
—Galatians 6:9

How much time do we waste looking for items that are missing in action—important things that become hidden within our piles of clutter? We dig through every kitchen drawer in search of that wire whisk. We rip through our desk, hunting for that magazine article we saved for a friend. And how often are we scrambling for our missing car keys or that wayward blue shoe?

Even just ten minutes of discombobulation a day would add up to over sixty hours a year of lost time—time we'd probably spend much more effectively and enjoyably if we thought about it. Surely, it's not that we don't value our time. Next to money, time seems to be what Americans long for most. Perhaps we just haven't considered the true cost of disorganization.

TIME SAVERS

1. *Have a central place (a basket or set of hooks) where you can always find your keys.*
2. *Make sure your filing system includes folders for magazine articles and newspaper clippings.*
3. *Buy multiples of identical socks so you can spend less time searching for mates.*
4. *Get a shoe rack or shoe shelf for your closet—and use it!*

PRAYER

Lord God, help me to realize that my earthly days
are numbered and my time here is valuable. Help me to organize
myself and my home so that I don't waste time. Amen

One Drawer at a Time

. . . and the waters gradually receded from the earth.
—Genesis 8:3

Okay, Rome wasn't built in a day, and we won't organize our homes overnight either. But we need to keep moving steadily forward—one baby step at a time. And we also need to celebrate every achievement along the way, whether it's something as monumental as cleaning the entire garage, or as seemingly insignificant as organizing our sock drawer.

The best way to ensure our continued success is to start with the smaller projects. And we're wise to focus our energies on the tasks that are most relevant and helpful to our normal day. While the garage clutter may be a problem, perhaps it doesn't hugely impair our ability to function. On the other hand, if we spend an inordinate amount of time getting dressed in the morning, it's likely our clothing-storage places could use some organizing and uncluttering.

CLOSETS 101

1. *Divide the clothes in your closet into two sections: those you wear, and those you don't.*
2. *If they are in good condition, give away the clothes you never wear.*
3. *Organize the clothes you do wear into groups (jackets, shirts, pants, skirts, etc.).*
4. *Separate the out-of-season items and store them until you need them.*
5. *Enjoy the feeling of more space and order, and know that if you can organize your closet, you can clean up the other cluttered areas of your home, too.*

PRAYER

God, remind me that baby steps are better than no steps at all.
Help me to keep moving forward. Amen

Pace Yourself

Great is our Lord, and abundant in power;
his understanding is beyond measure.
—Psalm 147:5

Suddenly, we're realizing that organizing and uncluttering our world is a really good thing—and not nearly as painful as we imagined. As we feel the power of getting control over this area of our lives, we may feel tempted to go overboard. Moderation is important now, yet for many of us, it's a challenge to live moderately on a regular basis. After all, we're the ones who overindulged in the first place. We accumulated too much stuff, and let it take over.

But instead of trying to eliminate our clutter and bad habits in one fell swoop, let's pace ourselves, and remember to enjoy each day for what it is. If we get into too big of a rush, we'll only make ourselves and those around us more miserable.

PACING POINTS

1. *Try to accomplish one small organizing task per day (like uncluttering one drawer), but forgive yourself for the days you miss.*
2. *Discipline yourself into breaking larger tasks into several steps to be done over a period of time.*
3. *Remember to take time for yourself to do something fun.*

PRAYER

Gracious Lord, help me to use my time wisely.
And remind me that that includes taking time
for people and pleasure. Amen

Why We Hang On

Search me, O God, and know my heart;
test me and know my thoughts.

—Psalm 139:23

Why do we hang on to stuff? The reasons we do what we do are as individual and unique as our thumbprints and DNA. Some of us cling to material things out of fear—we're afraid we'll be needy and wanting someday. Others simply lack the motivation to get rid of stuff as it accumulates. Some of us hold on to things because of a distorted sense of values—accepting worldly notions of what's important. Others truly believe our clutter is valuable. Some of us dislike change of any kind. And others lack the clarity to make decisions. The reasons are varied and many, but one lies within you. Ask yourself why you hang on to clutter. And then listen for the answer.

FOR FURTHER REFLECTION

1. *Does it seem you never have enough?*
2. *Do you place a great deal of importance on material things?*
3. *Is trusting God a challenge for you?*
4. *What might have led you to become a clutterer?*

PRAYER

Heavenly Father, help me to understand why I cling to my clutter.
Show me if there's a deeper problem that I need to address.
Help me to trust You with it. Amen

Confessions of a Clutter Queen

Indeed, what once had glory has lost its glory because of the greater glory.
—2 Corinthians 3:10

It's true. I am a clutter queen. My kitchen cupboards are crammed with empty yogurt and cottage cheese cartons, several incomplete sets of dishes, and all sorts of gadgets (I'm not even sure what they're for, but I keep them). My countertops (I can't remember their color) are piled high with several years' worth of junk mail, greeting cards, old photos (I plan to sort these someday), important newspaper clippings, valuable coupons (I plan to file if they're not expired), and an old pizza box or two (because, of course, it's hard to cook when I can't find anything in my kitchen!).

Is this really the proper environment for royalty? Would creatively considering how I could better store my clutter help me to sort it, and become more organized, and therefore use my things more effectively?

HOLD EVERYTHING

How might you use baskets, tubs, crates, and boxes to put similar loose items together in one easy-to-find place? Even tossing mittens, hats, and scarves into a cute wicker basket by the door instead of letting them pile up on the floor or creep all over the house would be a step in the right direction.

PRAYER

Dear God, I don't want to be a clutter queen anymore. Please, help me find creative ways to bring control and order into my life. Amen

Maybe No One Will Notice

My days are swifter than a runner;
they flee away, they see no good.

—Job 9:25

Time passes, and we may not think we are making significant progress in our uncluttering. Distractions come, interruptions occur, we are constantly derailed from accomplishing all those things we expected to have done (or at least started) by now. Were our goals unrealistic? Were we foolish to think we could change a way of life? Maybe we should just return to being content with the status quo. Maybe no one will notice anyway.

Okay, let's not kid ourselves. Even if we can train *our* eyes to overlook the clutter all around us, others will still see it. And our clutter sends the wrong message to observers. It tells them we're disorganized, unprofessional, or even lazy. Is this how we want to be perceived? Besides, let's be honest, don't we still long for a place of peace and order?

FOR FURTHER REFLECTION

1. *Can you forgive yourself for failing?*
2. *Can you acknowledge your accomplishments?*
3. *Set a new (small and attainable) goal for today.*
4. *Celebrate when you accomplish it.*

PRAYER

Lord, let me follow Your example of One who creates order,
not chaos. Help me to stay the course. Amen

Clutter Roots

For now we see in a mirror, dimly,
but then we will see face to face.
—1 Corinthians 13:12

We need to consider our roots, the way we were raised, and any genetic predispositions that may contribute to our habits. Were we raised in a family that cluttered? Did our parents grow up during the depression when every item was saved to reuse? Did they experience the war years when every scrap of tin foil, rubber, and glass was saved? It's possible these habits have been passed down to us. Or perhaps we are reacting to a very structured upbringing, where absolutely nothing was ever out of place in our homes when we were children.

We have to learn to let go. We can't allow the past to rule us. We must realize that we are our own persons; we make our own decisions; and we have to live our own lives. If our lifestyle is being impaired by how we were raised, it's time to cut ourselves off from those clutter roots. It's time to take responsibility for our own actions.

FOR FURTHER REFLECTION

1. *How were you raised?*
2. *How were your parents raised?*
3. *Are you ready to break the chain—cut the clutter roots?*

PRAYER
Almighty God, help me to live wisely.
Help me to acknowledge my past and the hold
it may have on my present. Show me how I can
make changes and move on. Amen

Excuses, Excuses

Therefore prepare your minds for action;
discipline yourselves; set all your hope on the grace
that Jesus Christ will bring you when he is revealed.
—1 Peter 1:13

Aren't we good at coming up with excuses for living amidst a sea of clutter and disorganization? "Life is just crazy right now." "My children make it impossible to have order." "If only I had a maid!" "I don't have enough places to put these things." "I'm waiting until I have time to do it *properly.*"

But excuses are a barrier to where we want to go; they are the shackles that keep us trapped in a cluttered world. We need to eliminate our excuses, our rationalizing, our justifications. We need to simply acknowledge our weakness in this area, and then continue forward, one slow but steady step at a time. Because as soon as we fall back on our excuses, we cease to move ahead. And before we know it, we're right back where we started. So, let's agree—no more excuses!

FACE THE FACTS

1. *Admit that you are a clutterer.*
2. *Promise yourself that you will no longer use excuses to ignore what needs to be done.*
3. *Confess to someone close that you have made this resolution.*
4. *Pray for help to become victorious in this area.*

PRAYER

I confess, Lord, that I make excuses when I feel overwhelmed,
but I realize my excuses are holding me back.
Help me to break free from my excuses. Amen

Do I Need Clutter Therapy?

Create in me a clean heart, O God,
and put a new and right spirit within me.

—Psalm 51:10

It's possible that some of us are so used to a certain way of living that we feel completely trapped and unable to change. And, if that's the case, we may need outside help. If we've honestly made a conscious effort to change, yet still feel we're getting nowhere, we may be dealing with a problem bigger than just cluttering. And, if so, we should look for another source of help.

But for most of us, it's just a matter of motivation and self-discipline. Yet, regardless of our problem, it's always helpful to get outside support and encouragement. Perhaps there's a friend working on this same issue who's looking for someone to partner with. Or we might even consider starting a clutterers' club. For, undoubtedly, there is strength and comfort in numbers. And it's good to know that we're not alone.

CLUTTERERS UNITE

1. *Evaluate how you're progressing in the area of uncluttering your life.*
2. *Make a commitment not to be isolated, and to seek any outside help that's needed.*
3. *Find a clutterer friend who wants to partner with you and encourage you.*
4. *Consider starting a clutterers' club where you can share ideas and resources.*

PRAYER

Loving Father, remind me that we all need each other.
Show me ways I can partner with friends
so we can grow together. Amen

Use It or Lose It

It is the Lord who goes before you.
He will be with you; he will not fail you
or forsake you. Do not fear or be dismayed.

—Deuteronomy 31:8

What's the worst that can happen if we get rid of something that we may need one day? Does it mean we'll have to make do without it, or borrow it from someone else, or even go out and purchase it again? How does this minor inconvenience compare with the idea of becoming free from the unnecessary clutter in our lives? Seems like a good trade-off, doesn't it? Besides, if we have to borrow something from a neighbor one day, we might strike up a new friendship.

So, it's time to apply the tough rule of "use it or lose it" to our uncluttering process. And as we're sifting and sorting through, it's good to remember how we accumulated these things, to feel a little remorse over money spent and wasted. And it's a good time to commit ourselves to not making these same mistakes again.

GETTING TOUGH

As you sort through your clutter, ask yourself if you've used an item in the last year. If not, away it goes—either to charity, the trash, or a friend or family member you know will want it. Or, if you can't quite part with it yet—to a box of things you'll reevaluate in six months.

PRAYER

Dear God, help me to make the right decisions
in clearing out things I don't really need.
Give me clarity and a sense of trust
as I move steadily forward. Amen

Making Time to Make Time

*When Moses saw that they had done all the work
just as the Lord had commanded, he blessed them.*

—Exodus 39:43

How often do we say, "I'd love to do that, if I could just *make* the time." But how do we make time? Perhaps it's in learning how to *save it*. And evolving into a more orderly person is a great way to save time. Just imagine the minutes, the accumulated hours, we can save as we continue to streamline our lives. But then we must learn to value and guard that precious time. And realizing how hard we worked to earn those extra moments might compel us to use them more wisely.

Another way to *make* time is to unclutter our schedules and our calendars. This can be achieved by combining tasks and errands so we can finish them in fewer trips, saving the run-around time. It also comes by simply saying "no" to time-consuming activities and events that aren't in our best interest.

TIME SAVERS

1. *Create shortcuts for repetitive tasks (like having two hampers to separate whites and darks; preprogramming your phone's speed dial; making a master grocery checklist to use and reuse).*
2. *Find your optimum productivity time (morning, noon, night?) and schedule more challenging tasks for those times, when you're at your best.*
3. *Learn to delegate time-consuming chores with a rotating work chart.*

PRAYER

*Eternal God, teach me how to save time.
And remind me to take time for rest and reflection. Amen*

Garage Sale Anyone?

Give no thought to your possessions,
for the best of all the land of Egypt is yours.
—Genesis 45:20

For those of us trying to get free of the clutter bug, being anywhere near a garage sale can be a big mistake. But if having your *own* sale encourages you to clean out your clutter in a more ruthless manner, then go for it. Just keep a few things in mind.

It takes a lot of time and energy to organize, run, and clean up after a garage sale. And unless you have some really big-ticket items, they aren't a surefire way to make money. It's really much easier to just box up your castoffs and take them to the Salvation Army. But another way to hold a garage sale is to partner with neighbors or friends. You might also consider having a charity garage sale where all proceeds are donated to your favorite worthy organization. Just remember a garage sale equals lots of work!

GARAGE SALE TIPS

1. Pick a season that works well for you and your region.
2. Sort, clean, organize, and price your "inventory" for fair garage sale market value.
3. Run an ad in the local paper, and get a sale permit if your town requires it.
4. Strategically place large, legible signs (with directions and hours) the night before.
5. Have paper and coin change in a box, calculator, phone, electrical outlets to try appliances, mirror for trying on clothing, and unlimited patience and willingness to bargain.
6. Prepare to have unsold items picked up after the sale.

PRAYER

Lead me, always, Merciful Lord.
And help me to have a charitable spirit. Amen

Who Wants to Be Superwoman?

Bless the Lord, O my soul.
O Lord my God, you are very great.
You are clothed with honor and majesty,
wrapped in light as with a garment.

—Psalm 104:1, 2

Who among us truly desires that everything in our homes run with clockwork precision? Most of us know that the "Superwoman" role comes with a hefty price tag. And most of us realize that to live our lives with the order and structure of Superwoman wouldn't really be all that satisfying or fulfilling. In fact, it might be a rather lonely existence. Not to mention, it could make us slightly nuts!

But wouldn't it be nice to walk into the laundry room without fear of being buried in an avalanche of clothes? So, perhaps it's time to admit that, although we're not superwomen, we do have the power to change—it resides in our own two hands. For we're equipped to do what needs to be done. It's simply a matter of choice—and sticking to the course we've set before us.

PLANNING AHEAD

Purchase a year's worth of greeting cards all at once. Address and stamp each envelope and file according to the month of the occasion. Then whenever a birthday or holiday rolls around, you can reach into your file and you're all set! Just write your greeting and send.

PRAYER

Help me, God, to accept my limitations.
But also help me to save time so I can
better use my personal strengths. Amen

When Things Rule Us

Do not worry about anything,
but in everything by prayer and supplication
with thanksgiving let your requests be made known to God.
—Philippians 4:6

Sometimes we allow material things to govern our feelings. We get frustrated when the vacuum cleaner breaks. We become angry when we open the refrigerator to find the milk's gone sour. And in the same way, we can allow our lack of organization to dramatically impact the way we live. Instead of ruling over the material things in our homes, we often allow those things to rule over, and sometimes even conquer, us.

We need to remember that *we are the ones in control here*. We make the decisions about whether we allow our clutter to accumulate or whether we deal with it immediately. We determine whether or not we have adequate groceries in the house to prepare a good dinner. We are not the victims of chance and circumstance. We are in charge! And it's time we realized it.

LABELS, LABELS, LABELS

If you want to find it again—label it. Whether it's a box of clothes, a container in a cupboard, or a file folder in a cabinet, if you want to retrieve its contents easily—label it. You might also label shelves in the linen closet, the pantry, or the garage, so everyone will put things back in their proper place.

PRAYER

Lord, help me to remember that things are simply things.
Teach me how to regain my control over them
instead of them taking control of me. Amen

Nearest and Dearest

And now faith, hope, and love abide, these three;
and the greatest of these is love.
—1 Corinthians 13:13

Sometimes we begin a campaign with such fervency and passion that we inadvertently step on a few toes along the way. And often those squashed toes belong to the people dearest to us—those we love the most. "But it's for their own good," we reason. And, besides, we can't change the world we live in all by ourselves—we need cooperation. But surely there must be some effective ways to get our family and friends on board without raking them over the coals.

Perhaps we should focus primarily on our own challenges (at least to start with) and then keep in mind how our own progress is a slow evolution. Then maybe we won't expect so much from others. And hopefully we can begin to teach by example. And finally, instead of focusing on someone's failure, let's celebrate their success (no matter how small). And let's always treat those around us the way we like to be treated.

AN EXERCISE IN LOVE

1. *Admit to your family and friends that you are trying to overcome an area of weakness.*
2. *Apologize for any overzealous or judgmental attitudes.*
3. *Invite them to partner with you, and to share their own ideas.*
4. *Encourage them by praising any efforts on their part.*

PRAYER

Dear God, remind me that nothing is more important than loving those around me. Show me how to repair relationships. Help me to be a good example. Amen

Grace for the Day

Grace to you and peace from God our Father.
—Colossians 1:2

What a relief that we need only live one day at a time. How overwhelmed we become when we try to predict or take on the problems that lie ahead of us. And in the area of bringing about order from chaos, one day usually contains enough trials of its own. But while each day holds plenty of challenges, God offers us sufficient grace to get through it. We just need to remember to ask.

We'd all do well to take a few moments at the beginning of each day and, quieting our minds, come before God and invite His gentle touch and sound direction onto the hours ahead. We can ask for His blessing of peace and order and wisdom to guide us through the upcoming day. For how can we expect to experience God's grace for the day if we forget to pause and ask? So, let's remember to come before Him, each morning, with great expectations.

A QUIET MOMENT

1. *Find a quiet spot where you can be alone.*
2. *Breathe deeply and allow your spirit to relax.*
3. *Thank God for how He cares for you.*
4. *Ask specifically for wisdom, direction, patience, or whatever you may need.*
5. *Take time to listen for His answer.*

PRAYER

Thank You, God, for always being there,
for always giving me grace for the day. Amen

Beyond the Door

To the one who conquers I will give a place
with me on my throne, just as I myself conquered
and sat down with my Father on his throne.
                                    —Revelation 3:21

Our homes, like our personal lives, often have spaces that we would like to remain locked and closed indefinitely. Perhaps it's because we're afraid for anyone else to see what's in there. Or maybe we just don't want to look ourselves. Or we might even be worried that once that closet is opened and the stuff spills out, we will never, ever, be able to sort through it all, not to mention put it in order and get it back in there again.

But we fail to realize the great reward that will be gained when we conquer that space. First of all, we may discover something important that we thought was lost. Next, we will find the task really wasn't as big and daunting as we had imagined. And finally, we will be pleased with the order and space we acquire when we're finished. So, what are we waiting for? Let's open the door!

TACKLING A BIG PROJECT

1. *Make sure you have enough time and energy to start something big (or plan how you can break it into phases).*
2. *Get your tools together (boxes, garbage bags, labels, hangers, cleaning supplies).*
3. *Ask yourself if this might require a team effort. (Is muscle involved?)*
4. *Plan a reward for when you are finished.*

PRAYER

Almighty God, help me to bravely conquer the places
(both physical and spiritual) that need cleaning and order.
Strengthen me to open that door. Amen

No Room at the Inn

Do not neglect to show hospitality to strangers,
for by doing that some have entertained angels
without knowing it.

—Hebrews 13:2

How many times have you used "I'm sorry, I just don't have the room . . ." as an excuse for not being more hospitable? And yet how many square feet do you have in your home? In Japanese cities, the average apartment has only about 300 square feet (the size of a large living room) and yet the Japanese are known throughout the world for their gracious hospitality. So, what's wrong with us?

Perhaps it's that we're allowing what space we do have to be occupied by inconsequential stuff—things that we don't really need, never actually use, and don't even like. Perhaps if we were willing to make some changes and get rid of some stuff, we'd have more room to create a pleasant space for guests. It's amazing how little room it takes to contain a futon and movable screen—and presto!—you have an instant guest area.

INGREDIENTS FOR A GUEST ROOM

1. *A comfortable bed with fresh sheets and plenty of blankets*
2. *A small bedside table (a storage box with a tablecloth thrown on top can work)*
3. *A reading light and clock (perhaps a couple of good books as well)*
4. *A set of fresh bath linens (perhaps a small basket of bath products)*
5. *A place for clothes (a chair or wall hooks if there's no closet)*
6. *Something that says welcome (fresh flowers, a candle, a small bowl of fruit)*

PRAYER

Gracious Lord, teach me to think hospitably.
Help me to open my home to others. Show me how to create
an attractive and welcoming space. Amen

Singing the Laundry Blues

Sing to him a new song; play skillfully
on the strings, with loud shouts.

—Psalm 33:3

They say there are two things in life that are inevitable—death and taxes. But what about the laundry? It seems that's something we can never escape either. And since we can't avoid it, perhaps it's time we learned to accept and conquer it. That is unless we want to spend the rest of our days singing the Laundry Blues. And everyone knows that song gets old after a while.

So, how might we streamline the process? For starters, how about a system for presorting? This can be as simple as having different hampers for different types of clothes. It's also helpful to keep all our laundry products handy, and to create a space for clean things (like a counter for stacking, or rods or hooks for hanging). But just as we're all unique, so too should be our laundry areas. They should accommodate our own particular needs and make our lives flow more easily.

LAUNDRY ROOM TIPS

1. *Develop a sorting system that works for you.*
2. *Dedicate a shelf, cabinet, or wire rack for soap, bleach, fabric softener, spot remover, spray starch, etc. (Make sure it's out of reach of small children.)*
3. *Install a rod or clothesline or put up hooks.*
4. *Clear off a counter or table for folding clothes.*
5. *Find a place to hang the ironing board and iron so they won't take up floor space.*

PRAYER

God, help me to tackle even the most mundane tasks
with wisdom, enthusiasm, and perseverance. Amen

A Losing Battle?

No, in all these things we are more than
conquerors through him who loved us.
—Romans 8:37

The problem with clutter is that once we've "solved the problem" it doesn't simply vanish forever. No, just like junk mail and telemarketers and a bad penny, it keeps coming back. But in order to keep this from being a losing battle, we must continue to contend against it. For in the same way our muscles become accustomed to an exercise routine that feels less strenuous over time, so we can also become accustomed to simply picking up and tossing out items before they transform into detrimental clutter. But the minute we let our guard down, we begin to lose that battle.

The good news is, even if we allow our clutter to get a little out of hand, we should be attaining the skills and knowledge to bring it quickly back under our control. That is if we don't wait too long. So, let's continue marching forward, picking up more tools and weapons along the way.

ELIMINATING A BIG CLUTTER MAKER

Send a stamped, self-addressed envelope to Mail Preference Service, Direct Marketing Association, P.O. Box 9008, Farmingdale, New York 11735, along with a note requesting a free "mail preference" registration form. This form lets you remove your name from any or all lists.

PRAYER

Help me, Lord, to remember that it's up to me
to stay on top of taming my clutter habits.
Help me to remain sharp in this area. Amen

Don't Throw That Away

Be still, and know that I am God!
I am exalted among the nations,
I am exalted in the earth.

—Psalm 46:10

How often do we say "I'd better not get rid of that because I might need it someday"? But to live in a continual state of holding on to things for fear we might miss out on something is to live in a prison of sorts.

Let's consider a dog who's been sadly neglected. He's got an old bone that's near and dear to his heart. Then someone comes along who wants to help the dog and care for him. She offers him some good, nutritious food, but the dog, unable to release that sorry old bone, can't enjoy more than a quick bite or two before returning to it. When we cling to the useless clutter in our lives, we too are missing out on something better. Important things like order and space! But perhaps the biggest thing we miss out on is the sweet inner peace that comes with trusting God for our provisions.

NATURE WALK

Take a walk outside and pay attention to the peace and order you see in nature. Consider how trees don't cling to their leaves in the autumn, because new, green ones will appear in the spring. See how roses aren't afraid to lose their velvety petals, for they will be replaced by fresh, vibrant buds. There's a healthy cycle in nature from which we can learn. An order where things come and go—a beautiful balance of life.

PRAYER

Lord, teach me to appreciate the way You created the world to be constantly refreshed and renewed. Help me to embrace this cycle of life within my own home. Amen

The Little Engine That Could

So I tell you, whatever you ask for in prayer,
believe that you have received it, and it will be yours.
—Mark 11:24

Remember the story of the Little Blue Engine? She had a challenging task to perform, but because she kept telling herself, "I think I can, I think I can, I think I can . . ." she was able to make it over the mountain. Nothing will defeat a clutterer more quickly than negative thinking. As soon as we succumb to hopelessness, despair, or apathy, we begin to suffer defeat. And we start slipping back down the mountain.

We need to embrace positive thinking. We need to tell ourselves, daily, "I think I can, I think I can . . ." and then, like that Little Blue Engine, we need to keep chugging steadily forward. We also need to remember to pause every now and then and instead of looking at how far we still have to go, glance back and celebrate how far we've already come. And then we can happily continue our trek up the mountain.

CONTAINING THE CLUTTER

Do a quick survey of the types of clutter that tend to accumulate in your home (reading materials, remote controls, toys, craft items). Then consider ways you can group like items together. How about a small covered box for remotes? Or a magazine crate? Maybe you need a reading basket for current books, reading glasses, notepad, and pens. Think of new ways to contain the necessary clutter.

PRAYER

Father, help me to think and speak more positively.
Show me how my thought patterns greatly impact the way I live.
Restore my hope. Amen

Recycling My Attitudes

Each of you must give as you have made up your mind,
not reluctantly or under compulsion,
for God loves a cheerful giver.

—2 Corinthians 9:7

One weakness clutterers tend to share is our difficulty in giving things away. And while we may understand that this weakness comes from all sorts of root causes, we can also discover that there is one foolproof cure. And that is to just start doing it. When we choose to give to others—whether it's the Goodwill store or the young couple across the street—we begin to experience the deep satisfaction of true generosity. And therein lies our cure.

For as our giving attitudes change (and our closets grow manageable) we begin to look for new and better ways to give. We learn to donate our time and talents, and from our pocketbooks, and best of all from our hearts. And before we know it, we are experiencing a lifestyle so rich and wonderful that we wonder what took us so long to get there!

RECYCLING TIPS

Every home's recycling needs differ. But to start with you need a recycling area that's preferably not a living area (think garage, laundry room, closet). Next you need appropriate containers to separate items (cans, glass, newspapers). And don't forget a specific marked box for items you plan to give to your favorite charity's thrift shop.

PRAYER

Lord God, change my way of thinking when it comes to giving. Help me to be more like You. And show me new and creative ways I can be actively generous. Amen

Is There Hope After Clutter?

And hope does not disappoint us,
because God's love has been poured into our hearts
through the Holy Spirit that has been given to us . . .
—Romans 5:5

Maybe you're still in the thick of your clutter battle, and perhaps you're even wondering if you will ever reach the end of this long, dark tunnel. But, while the fight to control clutter may seem endless, we must remember there is a great, big, wonderful reward for each of us when we arrive at the place where we're finally in control of our clutter—the time we realize that clutter is no longer controlling us.

And we can expect that reward to come in the form of additional space to live and breathe and function more easily. We can also look forward to a deeply satisfying peace from knowing that we have all we truly need *and* that we can find it when we need it! And then there's that tranquility that's the result of living in a habitat that is orderly and neat. Now, isn't that what we're all longing for?

LOST AND FOUND SPOT

Part of a family's daily clutter comes in the form of odds and ends like a wayward game piece, a single sock, a hair barrette, a baseball card, or a small toy. Get an attractive container (basket, decorative box, pottery jar) and place it in a designated "lost and found" spot. Make sure all family members get in the habit of putting "found" items in it, while checking there regularly for "lost" items.

PRAYER

Dear God, help me to look forward to the rewards
of living in a clutter-free home. In the meantime, help me
to persevere with a positive spirit. Amen

What You See Is What You Get

My people will abide in a peaceful habitation,
in secure dwellings, and in quiet resting places.
—Isaiah 32:18

As we continue to unclutter our homes, we will experience some related benefits in other areas of our lives, too. One of which is having a little additional time in our day. Because as we all know, we waste an awful lot of time continually sorting through piles of clutter in order to find what we're looking for. Clutter can be very distracting and plowing through it can be very time-consuming.

As we become more streamlined and organized we can begin to appreciate the value of finding and identifying things quickly. We may find ourselves relying on containers to hold and organize items we use on a regular basis, but the problem with containers is we don't always know what's inside—or we forget. And that can slow us down. So consider choosing clear containers for closets and cupboards, or using labels liberally. Then what you see will really be what you get.

VISIBLE CONTAINERS

1. *Gallon-sized glass jars (often available from school cafeterias) make great containers for dry kitchen goods. You can even spray-paint the lids for aesthetic appeal.*
2. *Clear "sweater" boxes can be used to store other things (craft items, small garden tools, sewing notions).*
3. *Many plastic containers have a clear strip down the center.*

PRAYER

Help me, Lord, to maintain a transparent heart
toward You as I continue in my battle against clutter.
Teach me to be wise. Amen

Change Is Good

A new heart I will give you,
and a new spirit I will put within you . . .
—Ezekiel 36:26

Many clutterers are naturally resistant toward change of any kind. We tend to think that change represents stress or demands that we're reluctant to face. But it's time to realize that change is a good and necessary element of life. Life without change would bring death. To remain alive and healthy, our bodies must constantly be in a state of change and renewal—cells are used up, die, and are replaced. Why should our habitat be any different?

And when we adapt our attitudes about change in regard to our habitat, we begin to enjoy a richer and fuller environment. We begin to make seasonal changes—a new candle to be burned and enjoyed, a fresh arrangement of flowers, a different set of pillows for the sofa (when we have the sense to get rid of the old ones!). And suddenly we begin to feel more fresh and alive ourselves.

COLOR TIPS

1. *Consider what color palettes most appeal to you—which colors make you feel good? Cool blues and purples, warm russets and golds, vibrant primary colors, soothing neutrals, soft pastels, comforting earth tones?*
2. *Use the colors you enjoy as accents (candles, pillows, throws, silk flowers).*
3. *Change these colors seasonally. For instance, if you like pastels, try using rose and mint for Christmas, lavender and pale yellow in spring, aquatic blues in summer.*

PRAYER

Thank You, God, for the way You are constantly
changing and renewing the world I live in. Help me
to embrace change with a grateful heart. Amen

Won't Somebody Help?

For we are God's servants, working together;
you are God's field, God's building.
—1 Corinthians 3:9

Being a Lone Ranger clutter-buster can be pretty overwhelming. And as the old saying goes, "many hands make light work." So, maybe we need to consider some new ways we can involve others in our household in our campaign against clutter. It's always best to invite the participation of others *after* we've developed and are following a workable plan ourselves. And there are a few steps we can take to make this group effort easier on everyone.

First, it helps to have the tools we need ready and easy to use. This could mean having boxes, labels, and trash bags on hand. Or keeping specific cleaning products together in a handy carryall container. Also, we need to know how to match the right person to the appropriate task. Even a four-year-old can sort basic craft items. And finally, don't forget to lavish on the praise (even if the job wasn't done *exactly* how you might have done it). Remember you're training your crew.

WORK CREW TIPS

1. *Always plan ahead (keep an ongoing list of specific jobs you think others in your household can do).*
2. *Consider hiring outside help for daunting or time-consuming tasks.*
3. *Keep a schedule, perhaps rotating, for regular household chores.*
4. *Plan a reward for everyone following a good group effort.*

PRAYER

Dear Lord, help me to delegate better. Remind me that everyone
needs a chance to participate in the "action."
Help me to praise everyone's efforts. Amen

Will My Children Be Warped?

Little children, let no one deceive you.
Everyone who does what is right is righteous,
just as he is righteous.

—1 John 3:7

Children can't help but imitate their parents—that is until they become old enough to rebel. But chances are, once the teen years pass, they'll still be impacted by the examples of their parents—both positively and negatively. But children can also learn good lessons from our mistakes, especially when we take time to correct our mistakes while our children are still watching.

And the learning doesn't stop there. Our children continue to be affected as they watch us change and build good habits to replace the ones that impacted our lives so negatively. Not only that, we can partner with our children to help them organize and streamline their own spaces. For even the sloppiest child appreciates being able to quickly put his hands on his favorite toy when he really wants it.

UNCLUTTERING THE TYKES

1. *To avoid mix-ups, try color-coding your children's toothbrushes, towels, storage containers, and bedding (allow each child to pick a color like red, blue, or yellow, that various items are easily found in). Then little Jenny knows if it's yellow, it's hers!*
2. *Make children's closets accessible with low shelves and closet rods they can reach.*
3. *Keep a clothes hamper in each child's room. Encourage them to take their bags when full to the laundry room, where they can learn to sort darks and lights.*

PRAYER

Heavenly Father, show me ways I can help my children
to build healthy habits. Help them to learn from my mistakes
and follow my good examples. Amen

Everything in Its Place

For I am about to create new heavens
and a new earth; the former things shall not be
remembered or come to mind.

—Isaiah 65:17

Okay, we've already accepted that we need a place for everything, but what if we're running short on room? How can we keep everything in its place if we simply lack space? Perhaps we need to remember the old "space vs. stuff" rule: if we truly don't have room for something, then maybe we just can't keep it. But if the item is a necessity and we're short on space, then we need to rely on some ingenuity to make room. It's time to think outside of the box!

Look around your home. There may be some hidden storage areas you've overlooked. Baskets and attractive containers can be stored atop cabinets, refrigerators, wardrobes, or on high decorative shelves. Also, long, flat plastic storage crates work well beneath beds. Find out where your space is hiding and consider your options.

SUPER STORAGE SAVERS

1. *A trunk doubling as a coffee table can contain things like photo albums, games, and puzzles.*
2. *A table covered with a floor-length cloth can hide a large item below.*
3. *Furniture with extra drawers and shelves can be used for storage.*
4. *A wardrobe is an attractive piece of furniture that provides additional storage space.*
5. *A bookshelf can also hold baskets, boxes, and pottery that double as storage containers.*

PRAYER

Dear God, help me to think creatively in my home.
And help me to continue moving steadily forward.
Thank You for the progress I've made so far. Amen

Admitting My Weakness

Likewise the Spirit helps us in our weakness;
for we do not know how to pray as we ought,
but that very Spirit intercedes with sighs too deep for words.
—Romans 8:26

We all have specific areas of weakness when it comes to our cluttering habits. Some of us are impulsive buyers. Others are compulsive shoppers. Some of us have trust issues. While others are simply unmotivated. Some may have trouble making decisions. And others are procrastinators. But whoever we are, and whatever our problems, we all need to be willing to acknowledge our weaknesses.

For instance, if we struggle with compulsive shopping, but do nothing to change, we'll continually be bringing more potential clutter into our homes. And if we don't deal with our procrastination habit, we'll never get the upper hand in our battle against clutter. So we need to be willing to look at our weaknesses and ask ourselves if we're doing all we can to be victorious in these areas. And perhaps we need to consider some outside resources for additional help.

FOR FURTHER REFLECTION

1. *Do your cluttering habits seem related to one specific area of your life?*
2. *Do you have a habit that seems impossible to break on your own?*
3. *Have you considered partnering with a friend who can help you?*
4. *Have other people noticed or pointed out an area of weakness in your life?*
5. *Are you willing to look for outside help in this area?*

PRAYER

Open my eyes, Lord, to my blind spots,
and help me to acknowledge my weaknesses.
Help me to change and grow. Amen

The Quick Fix

Welcome one another, therefore,
just as Christ has welcomed you, for the glory of God.
—Romans 15:7

While there's no sensible way to permanently unclutter our homes overnight, there are a few tricks that can quickly pull some semblance of order into our lives when we suddenly learn we're having company in the next hour. These are the times when we learn to truly appreciate things like plastic tubs and crates and laundry baskets—and an out-of-sight area to temporarily stash them!

This is also a time to appreciate the hope of brighter times ahead—days when we'll no longer need to rely on trickery. When we see how the "quick fix" clears counters, tables, and chairs—and suddenly everything looks shiny and clean—we start to feel better. And that's when we're ready to enjoy some quality time with family and friends without apologizing for our cluttered mess.

COMPANY'S COMING!

1. *The big sweep: Take a laundry basket through the living room, collect clutter, and store out of sight. Have family members claim later (possibly at a price).*
2. *Kitchen zapper: Use oven and dishwasher as hideaways unless you need to cook. In that case, use tubs, bags, or even pillowcases to quickly move clutter to another spot (for the time being only!).*
3. *Welcome fix: Check front door area for muddy shoes, skateboards, etc. Consider a storage bench where these items can be tossed inside for a quick cleanup.*

PRAYER

God, teach me to treat others as I like to be treated.
Help me to welcome friends and family, even on short notice.
Amen

I'm Too Busy

If any of you is lacking in wisdom, ask God,
who gives to all generously and ungrudgingly,
and it will be given you.

—James 1:5

Sometimes it feels as if we're going a hundred miles an hour but getting nowhere—fast! And maybe we tell ourselves we're just too busy to deal with clutter and chaos. We promise ourselves we'll take care of it "as soon as things slow down." But of course they never do. And perhaps our cluttering habits are part of the reason we're running so hard and accomplishing so little.

Let's take a look at our desks, our work areas, our closets. Are they sleek and efficient, or crazy and confused? Do we honestly think that the way we perform can be all that different from the environment we inhabit? The way we live affects us. Certainly there are times when immersed in a project, that a certain amount of messiness is inevitable. But when the mess slows us down or stops us, something is wrong.

BACK TO BASICS

To simplify your wardrobe, and therefore save dressing time, think basics. Classic (not trendy) pants, blazers, skirts, and shoes in traditional colors like navy, camel, gray, black, and taupe are the foundation of a basic wardrobe, along with blouses and tops in neutral colors like white, cream, or black. Secondary clothing items like vests, scarves, and various colored pieces are used to accent the basics. Relying on a good basic wardrobe saves both time and money.

PRAYER

Dear Lord, show me how to use my time more wisely.
Help me to feel like I'm in control of even simple things
like my closet. Amen

My Closet, My Heart

*. . . for the Father himself loves you,
because you have loved me
and have believed that I came from God.*
—John 16:27

The way we live is often representative of the way we feel. A lovely, sensible, serene lifestyle can signify a heart that's generally at peace. On the other hand, a life filled with chaos, confusion, and disorder can mean we're suffering beneath the surface as well. And a good way to check our emotional pulse is to take a quick look through our clothes closets.

Are we holding on to clothes that don't fit right? Styles that are dated? Colors that don't flatter? Do we keep shoes that pinch? Jeans that are too tight? And, if so, *why?* Is this what we think our lives are worth? That we are only valuable enough to wear shoes that hurt and pants that look bad? Is this how you would treat a beloved child? Let's learn to see ourselves as God sees us—his own precious children.

CLOSET SIFTING

Go through the clothes in your closet item by item and ask yourself if each piece feels good when you wear it, and if it looks good on you. If you cannot answer yes to both questions, you should seriously consider giving the piece away.

PRAYER

*Loving Father, teach me to value myself as You do.
Help me to trust You with all things and to exhibit
my internal worth by the way I live externally. Amen*

Isn't This Hereditary?

But we are not among those who shrink back and so are lost,
but among those who have faith and so are saved.
—Hebrews 10:39

Over a lifetime, a particular behavior can become so ingrained in us that we might actually believe it's part of our genetic makeup. And we might even try to use this as an excuse to continue that behavior—thinking, I can't help this, it's just the way I am. But to give in to this rationale is settling for a life that's less than we deserve. It's giving in to bondage.

So, let's allow ourselves the freedom to become new creatures on a regular, perhaps even daily, basis. Let's forgive ourselves for blowing it yesterday, and focus our energies on moving forward today. Let's ask God for grace and strength and wisdom and healing. And then let's believe that He will give them to us—abundantly!

A MASTER LIST

To save time, and unclutter your mind, start using a master list for everything you need to do (whether it's at work, or home, or for the PTA). Your list can be contained on something as sophisticated as an electronic scheduler or as simple as a small spiral tablet. What matters is that you use it, and continue to use it. Date your list each day, list new items, cross off old, move things that were not done yesterday to today. To start with, your list may look messy and confusing, but observe how it falls into a practical order the more you use it.

PRAYER

Almighty God, help me to break free from old habits
that I've known for a lifetime. Teach me not to make excuses
to fail, but to make success my goal. Amen

Clutter Homes and Gardens

He will yet fill your mouth with laughter,
and your lips with shouts of joy.

—Job 8:21

Welcome to Thelma Thumpernickle's home. Now watch your step as you come in the front door. Notice the pile of shoes to your left, particularly the wet sneakers sporting an interesting shade of green. Next we see the cardboard box of old newspapers, meant for recycling of course, but we dare any among you to pick up *that* soggy box. Pay special attention to the Christmas wreath on the door; isn't it amazing how fresh those boughs have remained clear into May? Oh, they're plastic, you say. How clever.

Note the lovely oak coatrack loaded with many layers of coats, all sporting their own jackets of dust. And next to this, a handy table for dropping your keys. And it looks like there might be keys in there somewhere—beneath the old catalogs, Christmas cards, overdue library books—and look, is that Fido's chewy bone? Yes, we've barely started our tour, but I'm sure you can see why we've featured Thelma's house in *Clutter Homes and Gardens* this month.

STORAGE 101

1. *Store frequently used items on lower shelves where you can easily reach them.*
2. *Don't overstack. Keeping stacks to three items is a good way to avoid constantly moving things to reach the one on the bottom.*
3. *Group similar items together: baking ingredients in one cupboard, videocassettes on one shelf, camera supplies in one box.*
4. *Store things close to where you use them: vacuum cleaner near carpeted area, bathroom cleaners in bathroom, bed linens near bedroom.*

PRAYER

Lord, help me to see the humor in my cluttering ways,
even as I try to change. Amen

Left Brain, Right Brain

This God—his way is perfect; the promise of the Lord
proves true; he is a shield for all who take refuge in him.
—2 Samuel 22:31

It's been scientifically proven that women are generally better at thinking from both sides of their brain than most men. Women, by nature, tend to be more right-brained (verbal and creative). But due to the numerous and varied tasks of running households, keeping children on track, and making it to soccer practice on time, perhaps they have learned to use the left side of their brains (analytical and systematic) as well.

This shows us that we humans are highly adaptable, and have perhaps an even greater capacity for organization than we realize. And maybe this is exactly what God intended when He created us with two unique sides of our brain—that we use them both! Could it be that He actually wants us to operate with a fully engaged mind, utilizing right and left as we need them? What a concept!

BOOKSHELF BLUEPRINT

1. *Arrange fiction books alphabetically by author.*
2. *Organize nonfiction books by subject matter (gardening, geography, history, parenting).*
3. *Create a larger shelf for oversized or art books.*
4. *Group cookbooks in kitchen.*
5. *Group videos, photo albums, children's books together on separate shelves.*

PRAYER

Loving Creator, help me to understand all the amazing potential
You have woven into me and to utilize it fully. Amen

Creative Clutter

Let your steadfast love become my comfort
according to your promise to your servant.

—Psalm 119:76

Could we go too far in our battle against clutter? Could we contrive a world so stark and barren and sterile that no one would want to live there? Possibly. Especially if we're of that overly zealous nature that goes from one extreme to another. And so, as in all things, we should strive for balance. For, without a doubt, there are some forms of creativity that might be misconstrued as clutter.

For instance, any good craft or art project comes with its own form of clutter. But how do we manage it before it takes over? And then there are certain styles of decor (Victorian, for instance) that tend to look slightly cluttered, but appealing. If that's a style we truly appreciate, by all means we shouldn't get rid of it. Let's just make sure it's manageable and attractively displayed for our enjoyment.

DECORATING HINTS

1. *Color can be key in keeping decor from looking cluttered. Various objects in the same color scheme can be quite harmonious.*
2. *Grouping similar items is attractive, but varying elements like size and texture adds interest.*
3. *Sticking to only one style (country, modern, Victorian) per room reduces the feeling of clutter and chaos.*
4. *Keep it simple to start. Focus on a single decorative item or color that you absolutely adore, and carefully and slowly introduce more elements.*

PRAYER

Gracious Lord, help me to develop my creativity
so that my home might be more comfortable,
inviting, and attractive to all who enter. Amen

I Deserve Better

Even though we speak in this way, beloved,
we are confident of better things in your case,
things that belong to salvation.

—Hebrews 6:9

A clutterer is someone who tends to settle for less than the best. They often think that more is better, and will sacrifice quality for quantity. For instance, a clutterer might go into a department store to purchase a navy blue cardigan sweater, but then, suddenly, she is distracted by a sales table heaped with sweaters that are fifty percent off! Naturally, there's not a navy one in the bunch, so she goes home with a hot pink pullover, a striped turtleneck, and a lavender V neck—all for the price she'd expected to pay for the navy cardigan.

The problem is, none of those sale sweaters look attractive on her or go with her new wardrobe plan. She has sold herself short. Is it because she didn't feel she was worth the full-priced sweater? We need to believe we are worth the effort it takes to live an organized life. We are worth having a wardrobe that works. We are worth living in a habitat that's pleasant and peaceful. We do deserve better. But we must choose better.

IN HIBERNATION

The change of season is the perfect time to sort and organize closets. Old trunks, seldom-used suitcases, large plastic units with lids, even large plastic garbage bags put into new, lidded garbage cans, all work well for storing off-season clothes and bedding. Smaller boxes can be stowed beneath beds, on high closet shelves, or in wardrobes. If off-season clothing is kept out of sight, make sure you list where the items are stored.

PRAYER

Dear Father, remind me of my value to You.
Help me to value myself in a similar way.
I know it will reflect back onto those around me. Amen

Against the Odds

By your endurance you will gain your souls.
—Luke 21:19

Have you ever noticed that as soon as we start moving in a positive direction, someone often comes along and says something like: "Ya know, most diets don't really work . . ." or "Most people usually quit exercising after just three days . . . "? These naysayers probably aren't fully aware of the toll their negative words can take on us. They may even think they're being helpful to enlighten us. But we need to learn to trust ourselves and guard our hearts against outside gloomy predictions.

One way to protect ourselves from the pessimistic influence of others is to keep quiet until the effect of change can be observed. Because, for most people, seeing is believing. Another way is to have a ready comeback—something light and nonconfrontational like: "Hey, what have I got to lose?" And then remind yourself of all the people who worked hard, who never gave up, and who were never sorry later.

CALENDAR CLUES

1. *Have only one calendar, centrally located, in your home, with enough room for everyone to write appointments and special days on it.*
2. *Always record everything on this calendar as soon as you know about it.*
3. *Bright Post-it notes can be helpful in calling attention to a particularly busy day.*
4. *Various ink colors can be used for different family members' appointments (Dad's blue, Mom's pink, Jimmy's green).*

PRAYER

*Dear God, help me not to be derailed by insensitive comments.
And remind me that I can come to You for strength
and encouragement. Amen*

Life Isn't Fair

For where there is envy and selfish ambition,
there will also be disorder and wickedness of every kind.
—James 3:16

Where did we ever get the idea that life should be fair? And what is fair anyway? Usually, we become most painfully aware that "life isn't fair" when we see someone else who seems to have it much better and much easier than we do. And, of course, we're usually only glimpsing this person's life for a split second, and even then we might only see whatever it is they want us to see.

When we compare our lot in life with others, we tend to observe through tinted glasses, and as a result our reality is skewed. That's when we cry out: "Foul play. Life's not fair." But perhaps if we could train ourselves to avoid comparisons, we might not feel so cheated. And then we might even learn to see things on a deeper level and begin to understand that no one's life is perfect and problem free. We might even discover some new compassion for those we thought had it made.

MULTITASKING 101

1. *While on the phone, scrub surfaces of counters, stove, refrigerator, microwave . . .*
2. *When passing through a room, collect clutter along your way.*
3. *Straighten the laundry room while waiting for a load to finish.*
4. *Turn your cleaning routine into aerobics and get a workout.*

PRAYER

Forgive me, Lord, for comparing and complaining.
Thank You for Your many blessings on my life. Amen

Neat Freaks Are No Fun

A soft answer turns away wrath,
but a harsh word stirs up anger.

—Proverbs 15:1

"Pick up your dirty glass!" "Don't put your feet up there!" "Hang up that coat!"

We've all heard these warnings before, and probably said them ourselves, perhaps even more times than we care to admit. But a nagging neat freak can get on anybody's nerves. And if we're guilty, we may want to take a look at why and whether it's doing us any good. Do we nag because we've done our 180° turn and now we want everyone else jumping on our bandwagon, too? Or is it because we're still struggling and floundering to keep our heads above water and we really need the help of others? Or perhaps we're secretly angry and we feel no one respects us or our efforts?

Once we face the root causes, we can then decide how best to proceed. But we need to recognize that, unless our goal is to alienate, nagging will get us nowhere fast. If we really want help, we need to encourage, empower, and even reward.

GETTING YOUR CREW ON BOARD

1. *Make sure everyone knows where your ship is sailing—to a peaceful paradise.*
2. *Make sure they know their roles and responsibilities—do you need a chart?*
3. *Make sure you use positive and encouraging language.*
4. *Make sure you offer some rewards or praise for a job well done.*

PRAYER

Loving Father, help me to treat my family
in a way that honors You. Let me learn from Your
kind and gracious example. Amen

Don't Worry, Be Happy

And can any of you by worrying
add a single hour to your span of life?

—Luke 12:25

Can you think of any problem where worrying improved the situation? Can our anxiety make things get better? Of course not! But how often we succumb to that trap. And as we work toward our goal of acquiring better organization skills and a more clutter-free existence, it's easy to get discouraged, and perhaps even become plagued with new worries. "Will I ever be able to conquer this problem?" "Will there ever be an end to this clutter madness?" We can be overwhelmed with anxiety—especially as we delve deeper into our clutter habits, and start to realize just how widespread they may be.

But instead of focusing on what's wrong with where we've been, why not focus on what's right with where we're going? Why not rejoice that we have brighter days ahead? Why not celebrate that we're alive and well and moving forward today? And, here's the bonus, when we exchange our worry for happiness, we become much more successful and productive people. We realize our goals much sooner.

KITCHEN SPACE SAVERS

1. *Use cup hooks to hang mugs and cups above dishes.*
2. *Consider specially designed "under the cabinet" appliances to free up valuable counter space.*
3. *Store large, seldom-used appliances away from prime counter space.*
4. *Consider hanging pots from a rack.*

PRAYER

Almighty God, help me to bring my anxieties and
worries to You. Teach me to foster a positive attitude,
and give me hope for the better days coming my way. Amen

Can't We Just Ignore It?

Open my eyes, so that I may behold
wondrous things out of your law.

—Psalm 119:18

As clutterers, we made ourselves experts in the art of ignoring things—well, at least those things we didn't *want* to see. How many times did we walk past the same old stack of magazines without even seeing them, not to mention that layer of dust on top?

But there comes a day in every clutterer's life when he can no longer ignore these things. Maybe it's an inevitable point of consciousness. Or maybe it's just our fastidious neighbor turning up her nose when she walks through our kitchen. But the time comes when we can no longer turn away. Like a smoker who's given up cigarettes and finds their nose suddenly works with startling precision, so we begin to notice all those obnoxious things we used to simply ignore. But even so, we still need to pace ourselves.

A TIMED UNCLUTTERING EXERCISE

1. *Choose a task that should take about thirty minutes—like organizing beneath a sink, cleaning out a kitchen drawer, or straightening a cosmetics holder.*
2. *Get your necessary tools together (cleaners, garbage bags, give-away box, dust rags—whatever is appropriate to the task).*
3. *Set a timer for thirty minutes, and let the fun begin.*
4. *You should be done when the timer goes off; if not, finish up.*
5. *Reward yourself by enjoying how much better that area looks.*

PRAYER

Thank You, Lord, for opening my eyes
to all that's around me. Help me to see not only the problems,
but also the improvements. Amen

It Keeps Coming Back

Rejoice in hope, be patient in suffering,
persevere in prayer.

—Romans 12:12

Yes, it's true, clutter is one of life's continually recurring challenges. And just when you think you've got it whipped, your mother-in-law is sure to drop by with a trunk load of memorabilia that she's certain your children can't live without (actually, she's probably uncluttering her own house that day). And for that reason, we all need to realize this is one of those habits we can't take a break from without suffering some form of backlash.

Let's not deceive ourselves, thinking that "once this is done" we can just sit back and take it easy. For, just as the grass must be regularly mowed, so must clutter be regularly managed. But, if we're smart, we'll teach ourselves to appreciate this process (and its benefits!) and to continually pick up new tricks along the way.

INNOVATIVE STORAGE SITES

1. *Consider screening off an area and placing an open-shelf storage system there.*
2. *Hang an attractive floor-length curtain across a corner and use the space behind it for a stack of crates or boxes.*
3. *Look for any unused niches and consider what furniture items (like wardrobes, trunks, small dressers, or bookshelves) could be placed there to double as storage units.*

PRAYER

Dear God, strengthen me and teach me to persevere.
Remind me that self-discipline is a quality that
positively impacts many areas of my life. Amen

Call in the Experts

Listen to advice and accept instruction,
that you may gain wisdom for the future.

—Proverbs 19:20

Some of us may reach a point in our organizational efforts when we realize that we cannot possibly accomplish our goals on our own. Whether it's due to the demands of caring for young children, holding down a taxing job, or even facing a physical challenge, the time may come when we know we need to look outside of the home for help. And there are several ways to accomplish this.

We can consider job swaps. If we have a friend who's a super organizer but hates to cook, we might offer to cook a few meals in exchange for some organizing help. Or maybe we'll consider having a housekeeper come in weekly, or a window washer once a month. But let's not be afraid to consider help for whatever tasks seem too overwhelming to us and our schedules.

GETTING HELP

1. *Determine what sort of help you need (make a list, then prioritize).*
2. *Ask friends for recommendations for good help (personal references are always best).*
3. *Make a specific list of what and how you want things done.*
4. *Have the necessary tools handy.*

PRAYER

Heavenly Father, help me to recognize when and how
I may need assistance. Teach me not to be too proud to ask.
And bring the right helpers my way. Amen

Who Really Cares Anyway?

In your steadfast love you led the people
whom you redeemed; you guided them by your strength
to your holy abode.

—Exodus 15:13

Some of us may live alone, or with people who don't really seem to appreciate orderliness. And perhaps the idea of cleaning out all this accumulated junk may suddenly seem like an exercise in futility. After all, we may wonder, who really cares about how we live anyway? Is it really worth all this effort? This is a good question, and worthy of an honest answer.

But instead of asking if "this" is really worth the effort, perhaps we need to restate the question and ask ourselves if "we" are worth the effort. After all, is it unhealthy, or unsafe, or stressful for us to live in a cluttered and disorderly habitat? And if we can say yes to any of the above, then perhaps we need to realize that we are putting forth this effort because *we* care. And that we are important enough to keep going in a good direction.

A WELL-STOCKED CORRESPONDENCE PACK

1. *A covered box, basket, or desk drawer*
2. *Generic note cards, thank you cards, invitations, postcards, stationary, envelopes*
3. *Postage stamps, return address labels (or rubber stamp)*
4. *Address book, good writing pens, decorative stamps*

PRAYER
Dear God, remind me that I am worthy of having
a healthy and happy habitat. Show me ways
I can use my home to bless others. Amen

The Battle of Mail

Keep your heart with all vigilance,
for from it flow the springs of life.

—Proverbs 4:23

There's no stopping it. Come rain or sleet or hail or snow . . . one of the most regular ways clutter sneaks into our homes is through the U.S. Postal Service. And while much of our daily mail is greatly appreciated, a significant—and growing—portion is not. And even when we try to slow down junk mail delivery by contacting the correct sources or even returning it, it's difficult to stop this onslaught completely. So, perhaps it's better to simply attack it head-on and sort our mail as we stand over a wastebasket!

But even then, we often hold on to something we think might have some value: an interesting new catalog, a "free" offer, or a promising coupon book. But, as with all things destined "not to become clutter," these items should have a specific place in our homes—a place where we can put them and find them, to use or to toss, as needed.

TEMPORARY HOLDING AREAS

1. *If you use coupons, consider a small box with a filing system. But remember, coupons must be sorted and redeemed on a regular basis or they are worthless.*
2. *A catalog basket—used only to store catalogs—and cleaned out regularly*
3. *A correspondence rack—for letters that need answers, file most important in front*

PRAYER

Thank You, God, for the people who so faithfully deliver my mail each day. Help me to stay on top of small, daily tasks like sorting and disposing of junk mail. Amen

Daily Choices

And every day in the temple and at home
they did not cease to teach and proclaim
Jesus as the Messiah.

—Acts 5:42

Once we get a good sense of control over our cluttering problems, it probably won't undermine us to miss a day or two, here and there, along the way. Or will it? The trouble with allowing ourselves some occasional slack time is that it slowly creeps into our way of thinking and before we know it, we're beginning to feel overwhelmed again. Maybe this is because the general nature of a clutterer is to feel like we're always behind, always buried, always digging our way out.

Just as a jogger who's accustomed to his daily five miles suddenly feels like he's running uphill after missing a few days, so we'll feel discouraged and beaten if we allow ourselves to fall behind. And for that reason alone, it makes sense to stay on top of the game, to stick with our program and reinforce our already established good habits as we continue to make healthy daily choices.

POST-IT TIPS

1. *Keep a Post-it pad and a pen on a string stuck to the refrigerator for quick notes.*
2. *Post a note on the door for a visual reminder of dentist appointments, picking up the dry cleaning, meetings, etc.*
3. *Post a note on the bathroom mirror to remind you of a new medication, positive thinking, etc.*

PRAYER

Eternal Lord, remind me that life is a daily thing.
Help me to build and maintain good daily habits and disciplines.
Teach me to come to You for strength and grace. Amen

The Clutter Blues

O Lord, all my longing is known to you;
my sighing is not hidden from you.

—Psalm 38:9

Whether our problems stem from being overwhelmed by clutter or from the everyday demands of living in the twenty-first century, we all get the blues sometimes. But for those of us with a history of cluttering, we might react to the blues in a different way—sometimes a harmful way. For instance, some clutterers may think they can chase away the blues by going shopping. And a clutterer shopping with the blues is usually a big mistake.

Enticed by cheerful lights, pleasant music, tempting price reductions, and helpful salespeople, a clutterer can really get into trouble. In fact, it's under those conditions that we usually come home with a carload of items we never intended to purchase. And, without even addressing the wallop a trip like this can deal to our pocketbooks, these are the very items that are destined, within the next six months, to turn into clutter.

CLUTTER-BLUES BEATERS

1. *Call a clutter-keeping friend for support.*
2. *Take a nature appreciation walk.*
3. *Go to the library and find a good book.*
4. *Nurture yourself with a bubble bath and candles.*
5. *Rent an old feel-good movie.*
6. *Spend some time meditating on God's blessings on your life; make a thank you list.*

PRAYER

Gracious God, thank You for giving me the capacity
to feel a wide range of emotions. Show me some positive
and helpful ways to deal with the times I am down. Amen

What You Don't See . . .

Therefore we will not fear, though the earth
should change, though the mountains shake
in the heart of the sea . . .

—Psalm 46:2

Perhaps one of the best rewards of clutter-free living is the peace that comes from knowing you can open any closet door or any drawer, or peek into any hidden space, and not be horrified. For it's those untamed, unseen areas that really seem to haunt us. Perhaps it's because we imagine them to be in far worse condition or much more daunting than they really are. Maybe it's a fear of the unknown, the terror of the unseen. But whatever you call it, it can paralyze us.

Because what we don't see can transform itself into anything. It can kill us. And yet, when we fling open those doors, when we pull out our swords (or brooms) and attack and conquer what lies behind them, we emerge feeling empowered, ignited, victorious. It's like bravely stepping into the dark and gloomy cave, and slaying the ferocious dragon. We become the mighty liberator— our own hero!

A HANDY MA'AM TOOL BASKET

Find a large, sturdy basket with a handle for easy carrying. Fill with basic tools such as hammer, pliers, Phillips and regular screwdrivers, an assortment of nails and screws, measuring tape, carpenter's glue, scissors, adhesive tape, picture frame wire, sandpaper, and whatever else you need for simple household repairs.

PRAYER

Almighty God, strengthen me to face whatever
comes my way. Teach me to come to You whenever
I am afraid or overwhelmed. Amen

An Honest Moment

Rid yourselves, therefore, of all malice,
and all guile, insincerity, envy, and all slander.

—1 Peter 2:1

Perhaps we've reached a place in life where we're willing to examine ourselves and our thinking more closely. Maybe we're even beginning to suspect that our habit of accumulating clutter might be directly related to how we feel on the inside. Is it possible we could have some interior places that need to be cleaned and organized as well? For instance, we might be holding on to some old hurt that's never fully healed. Maybe we've clung to some unrealistic expectation that's now making life miserable. Or we might have shoved back some old bitterness against someone we really need to forgive.

Maybe it's time to start uncluttering our hearts. Do we have some doors that need to be opened wide? Can we shed some light inside? Expose some things that need to be removed from our lives? Are we ready to be free of some emotional clutter?

FOR FURTHER REFLECTION

1. *Take some quiet time to prayerfully ask if you have some unresolved emotional baggage cluttering up your heart.*
2. *Ask God to cleanse, forgive, and heal you.*
3. *Forgive yourself; envision yourself as clean and whole before God.*
4. *Forgive anyone else who may have inflicted hurt upon you.*
5. *Consider seeking additional help (good friend, minister, counselor) as needed.*

PRAYER

Merciful Lord, reveal any emotional clutter that I'm carrying within my heart. Help me to bring it to You for healing and cleansing. Amen

Outta Control

Fathers, do not provoke your children,
or they may lose heart.

—Colossians 3:21

The only person we can really, truly control (and *that* can often be a challenge) is ourselves. And sometimes that can make us feel as if the rest of the world is outta control! Well, at least, out of *our* control. And it can feel especially out of control when the people we live with don't hold to our standards, or they question our values, or totally ignore our examples. And, while these kinds of people can be found in all sizes and shapes, we usually call them teenagers. And they can definitely make life feel like it's outta control!

For that reason, these are the years when we really need to feel a sense of personal control and peace. And having an organized and fairly clutter-free existence can be worth a lot in the area of stress relief. Even when it feels like a teenager is living on the brink of chaos, we can derive some sense of serenity in maintaining a manageable habitat. And the teen years, like all trials and tribulations, shall also pass.

KEEPING THE PEACE

1. *Keep expectations to a minimum within a teen's domain (their room).*
2. *Maintain simple rules (for health and safety). If they wallow in their own mess long enough they may choose to clean up their act. Otherwise, just close their door.*
3. *Enforce cleaning rules (for health and sanity) within your domain (rest of house).*
4. *Pray for patience. And pick your battles carefully.*

PRAYER

Dear God, strengthen me for all life's challenges.
Remind me that I cannot control others. Show me new ways
to live in harmony with those around me. Amen

Clutterers Anonymous

Like a city breached, without walls,
is one who lacks self-control.

—Proverbs 25:28

For some of us cluttering is a recently learned habit, for others it is an established pattern, and for many it is an actual addiction. For just as some people are addicted to food, alcohol, or gambling, we can become addicted to clutter. And it's healthy to acknowledge this possibility so we can be aware that this might be, and most likely is, a lifelong challenge—an area where we never want to let our guard down.

Because before we know it, instead of a single empty cologne bottle on our dresser, we have sixteen. Instead of just a couple of old magazines on the coffee table, that coffee table is completely covered in them. When we leave ourselves wide open and vulnerable, clutter can slip in and catch us unaware. Perhaps one day we'll have a website for recovering clutterers to chat, encourage, and support one another. In the meantime, we might find solace as we unite with friends who, like us, continue to fight the war on clutter.

CLUTTERER SAFETY TIPS

1. *Never go shopping without a list.*
2. *Never go shopping for stress relief, or when you are blue.*
3. *Avoid garage sales (or if you must go, take a list).*
4. *When you bring something "new" into the house, make sure something "old" goes out.*

PRAYER

Father, help me to not become discouraged
about my cluttering ways. But also help me to learn how
to control this habit. Amen

A Twelve-Step Program

It shall be said, "Build up, build up, prepare the way,
remove every obstruction from my people's way."
—Isaiah 57:14

1. I admit I cannot control all circumstances in my life.
2. I believe that God controls the universe and wants to interact with me.
3. I make the decision to surrender my life and my will to God.
4. I make the decision to take a long, honest look at my life.
5. I admit to cluttering, clinging, and overlooking.
6. I make a commitment to unclutter and simplify my life.
7. I make a commitment to put away, give away, and throw away more stuff.
8. I make a commitment to clean out, organize, and enjoy my habitat more.
9. I seek through prayer and meditation to increase my contact with God.
10. I make a commitment to reach out to and interact more lovingly with those dear to me.
11. I make a commitment to forgive myself and others who've hurt me.
12. I make a commitment to share what I've learned with others who are held hostage by clutter.

CLUTTER-FREE COMMITMENT

Copy these twelve steps down (edit them as you see fit) and post them where you can see them regularly. Remember it's your life and you deserve to live in a clutter-free environment where a sense of serenity and order becomes the norm.

PRAYER

Dear Lord, help me to make and to keep my commitment to conquer clutter. Amen

Where Do I Sign Up?

But those who look into the perfect law,
the law of liberty, and persevere,
being not hearers who forget but doers who act—
they will be blessed in their doing.

—James 1:25

Wouldn't it be a relief if we actually could join a Clutterers Anonymous group? We could have some great motivational speakers lead us through drills that would ensure our success. Perhaps there might even be someone who would slip over for an unscheduled home inspection, doling out rewards for passing and demerits for flunking. Or maybe not.

As with most things in life, the accountability factor is usually found in the face we see in the mirror each morning. Sure, there might be friends and family who check in on us, but can they really make us do anything we honestly don't want to do? Not usually. And so, once again, it's that old self-discipline, that same stuff that gets us out of bed each morning, that we need to kick into gear. And we're the only ones who can do it.

LITTLE HABITS TO LIVE WITH

1. *Make your bed as soon as you get up.*
2. *Do the dishes (or load the dishwasher) as soon as you're finished eating.*
3. *Toss the newspaper or magazine as soon as you're done reading it.*
4. *Put your dirty clothes directly into the hamper.*

PRAYER

Strengthen me, God, to continue persevering in my attempts
to develop good habits. Help me to realize that what seems
like work reaps big rewards in my life. Amen

A Clean Heart

*But store up for yourselves treasures in heaven, where neither moth
nor rust consumes and where thieves do not break in and steal.
For where your treasure is, there your heart will be also.*
—Matthew 6:20, 21

It would be incredibly unfortunate if we successfully straightened, cleared, and uncluttered our physical habitats, creating lovely spaces that were clean and neat and orderly, but during the process completely neglected our interiors—our hearts. Because, as much as we need to keep up with those habits that affect the places we work and live, we need to care for our hearts even more.

Imagine that someone has a gorgeous, picture-perfect house and yet her heart is bitter and broken—as cold as stone. What good is an organized home—all set for entertaining—when no one feels welcome there? So, let's remember to keep our priorities in order. If our hearts are the place where God dwells, the place our inner spirit lives, how vital it is that we keep them clean and clear. And how important that we ask God to help us.

A DAILY SPIRITUAL CHORE

1. *Present your heart, your life, to God.*
2. *Ask God to show you if there is anything inside you that needs maintenance.*
3. *Ask God to forgive you, cleanse you, and guide you in His ways.*
4. *Thank God for His touch and blessing on your life.*

PRAYER

*Heavenly Father, remind me how important it is
that I come to You regularly and allow You to do Your work in me.
Help me to keep my heart honest and open to You. Amen*

An Orderly Mind

*Brothers and sisters, do not be children in your thinking; rather,
be infants in evil, but in thinking be adults.*
—1 Corinthians 14:20

Does our thinking affect our environment, or does our environment affect our thinking? Probably both. But just as we're training ourselves to roll up our sleeves and physically get in there and unclutter our habitats, we should also be training our minds to think in a more clutter-free way. And it's amazing how one really does impact the other. Imagine you're about to embark on a challenging research project—but your desk is totally buried beneath heaps and piles of papers, books, clippings, magazines, office tools, you name it—does this scenario inspire you to buckle down and work in an orderly fashion?

But when we've cleared the surface, filed things where they go, have the tools we need nearby, but not cluttering our space—suddenly our thoughts feel less jumbled. It's as if we can take a deep breath and really focus. Ah, the potential of an orderly mind!

SETTING UP A HOME OFFICE

1. *Consider light—do you enjoy natural sunlight, or are you a low-light person?*
2. *Does the area you're considering feel pleasant, warm, inviting?*
3. *Is there access to electrical outlets and phone jacks?*
4. *How much space do you need? Full desk? Computer station? Just a niche?*
5. *Do you need to be near windows, or do they distract you?*
6. *Do you work better in isolation, or do you prefer to feel the energy other people generate?*

PRAYER

*Dear God, I long to have a sharp and orderly mind.
Please help me to improve my thinking habits. Amen*

Room to Breathe

But the Lord answered her, "Martha, Martha,
you are worried and distracted by many things; there is need of
only one thing. Mary has chosen the better part,
which will not be taken away from her."
—Luke 10:41, 42

So, suddenly, we look around us and we realize that things are improving. Spaces are becoming more cleared and open, life is becoming more functional. A sense of order is slowly starting to slip into place. And we can see that we have *room in our lives!* We may even have some spare time. And, at first, the temptation might be to fill up these spaces and slots. We may begin dreaming up things and activities that we can shove right back in there—but wait a minute!

Before we start filling up what we've worked so hard to clean and clear, why not just give ourselves a break? Take a moment to breathe deeply, enjoy the new room in our lives, and just relax a little. And before we make any decisions to bring in one single thing, let's ask ourselves *why?* And let's remember one big uncluttering goal was to create some space and peace and serenity. So let's not start cluttering it back up.

TAKE TIME

1. *Take time to look around and enjoy what you are creating.*
2. *Take time to think and dream of where you'd like to be.*
3. *Take time to be hospitable, to share your improving habitat with others.*
4. *Take time to nurture and reward yourself for the progress you've made.*

PRAYER

Lord, teach me to appreciate calmness, serenity,
a sense of well being, and to enjoy peace and quiet. Amen

Uncluttering the Pocketbook

I signed the deed, sealed it, got witnesses,
and weighed the money on scales.
—Jeremiah 32:10

As we get a better handle on organizing the larger areas in our lives, we begin to notice some of the smaller areas, too. Like after you mop the floor and then suddenly realize that the baseboard also needs a good scrubbing. But one seemingly small area is extremely important, and left to itself can turn into a gigantic nightmare. And that is the area of finances—or bill paying. Unfortunately this is something that also comes with its own little pile of clutter. But it too can be controlled.

One of the first ways to tame finances is to have one designated person in charge of them. This person deposits checks, pays bills, and balances the checkbook. And having a well-organized but simple-to-use filing system will prevent oversights and frustrations.

A SIMPLE BILL-PAYING SYSTEM

1. *When bills arrive, open and dispose of exterior envelopes, then stamp and put your address label on return envelope.*
2. *Temporarily place these unpaid bills in an open rack or file system, according to the date due. This allows you to pay them as they're due, or monthly.*
3. *As you pay bills, drop bill stubs (and bank statements) into an expanding folder system, organized by month.*

PRAYER

Almighty God, help me to live responsibly when it comes to money. Help me to get my finances in good order. Amen

Yearly Tasks

Sow for yourselves righteousness; reap steadfast love;
break up your fallow ground; for it is time to seek the Lord,
that he may come and rain righteousness upon you.
—Hosea 10:12

Thank goodness, there are some tasks that need to be done only once a year. Things like cleaning the gutters, packing away Christmas decorations, or doing taxes. But even these daunting tasks can become less intimidating when we've done some uncluttering and established a sense of order. For instance, it's a lot easier to put up storm windows when you can easily find them in your orderly garage, and your window-cleaning supplies are all in one bucket, and you know exactly where your tools are located. You can probably save at least half the time you used to spend on the job.

And taxes are no different. If we set up and utilize an organized system throughout the year, it becomes that much quicker and easier to file in April—or, hey, maybe we'll file in January this year!

TAX TIPS

1. *Use an accordion file with slots for all deductible categories that you use (business expenses, charity, home improvements, investments, IRA's, mortgage, medical). Drop stubs and canceled checks in appropriate pockets throughout the year.*
2. *Use only one designated credit card for all deductible expenses.*
3. *Keep a mileage journal for business travel.*
4. *Keep a journal of any deductible investments, with a pocket for receipts.*

PRAYER

Dear God, help me to fully realize how a little effort toward organization now can pay off big dividends throughout the year.
Amen

Avoiding Holiday Turmoil

The saying is sure and worthy of full acceptance,
that Christ Jesus came into the world to save sinners . . .
—1 Timothy 1:15

Even the most recovered clutterer can feel challenged as holidays roll around. Especially at Christmastime when the temptation to accumulate more stuff than anyone needs borders on madness. But perhaps we can prepare ourselves for this onslaught of consumer-targeted commercialism. And maybe, by intentionally willing ourselves to scale down, simplify, and even eliminate previously collected clutter, we might actually enjoy one of our best Christmas experiences ever.

Because we all know that Christmas isn't about stuff. It's about loving one another and giving from the heart (not the pocketbook). It's about spending joyous, quality time with family and friends (not being stressed out from too much shopping). It's about taking time to remember the sweet simplicity of that first Christmas so long ago.

HOLIDAY SANITY SAVERS

1. *Go through your Christmas decorations and put all those you no longer use in a giveaway box. Store the rest in well-marked boxes, perhaps organized by the rooms they are used in.*
2. *Do not Christmas shop without a specific list, and do not shop during rush times.*
3. *Keep holiday plans simple. Focus your energy on people, not on things.*
4. *Don't fall into a holiday guilt trip. Do only what you're able to do cheerfully.*

PRAYER

Loving Father, help me to be prepared for the holidays.
Remind me to celebrate what really matters—things like love,
peace, and joy, and the birth of Your son. Amen

Gifts with Heart

You show me the path of life. In your presence there is fullness of joy; in your right hand are pleasures forevermore.

—Psalm 16:11

All year long we are hit with gift-giving occasions: birthdays, baby showers, graduations, Mother's Day, Father's Day, and so on. And giving is a good thing—especially when we can do so with a cheerful spirit. But sometimes we're running short on time, heavy on guilt, and we don't always make the wisest decisions. This is a case where a little prevention is worth a lot of cure.

First, take a look at the remaining year, starting from whatever month it is right now. Naturally, you get this information from your one, centrally located, calendar. Chart the months ahead in a "gift log" (a small notebook) which you will keep under lock and key—or in your purse. Write down every birthday and gift-buying event that you can think of right up until Christmas, leaving a blank space where you will fill in the gift later. This log will be handy for years to come: It helps you plan ahead, and it records past gifts—so you can look back and see that you gave Dad a tie on his *last* birthday.

MAKING A LIST AND CHECKING IT TWICE

1. *Use your gift log to buy or make specific gifts well in advance.*
2. *Take advantage of great sales prices for basic gifts that work for baby showers, secret pals, weddings, children's birthdays, etc. List these in the "generic" section of your log and check it when an occasion pops up unexpectedly.*
3. *Appropriately wrap gifts and use Post-its to list contents or names.*
4. *Store until needed in a secret stash area (closet, high shelf, or cabinet where you have some extra room and aren't worried about little eyes peeking).*

PRAYER

Dear Lord, help me to see what joy there can be in giving when it's stress free and from the heart. Amen

A Daily Discipline

Do not let loyalty and faithfulness forsake you; bind them around your neck, write them on the tablet of your heart.

—Proverbs 3:3

As we become more organized, we naturally have more time, but we still want to protect those extra minutes. We still need to enjoy and treasure that bit of breathing room. But one activity we might wish to consider—something that promises to greatly enrich our lives—is journaling. For writing in a diary or journal is more than just a way of tracking how we spend our days (although it's great for that). It's also a way to express and consider our thoughts, and a way to better understand and deal with our feelings.

Writing in a journal is never a waste of time. We can record our concerns, write out heartfelt prayers, contemplate solutions, make lists, write poetry, count our blessings—all sorts of things. And, on top of everything else, the act of writing is just one more way to organize our thoughts and unclutter our minds.

JOURNALING 101

1. *Get a notebook that feels comfortable to use, and commit to using it.*
2. *Go easy on yourself at first. Perhaps just say something about the day, what you want to accomplish, or what you did yesterday.*
3. *Do not attempt to edit yourself or become critical; this will only shut you down.*
4. *Allow creativity to emerge however it likes, in poetry, humor, ideas, lists, whatever . . .*
5. *Remember your journal is for your eyes only. Store it safely away from everyone else.*

PRAYER

*Dear God, teach me to value my thoughts and my mind.
Help me to be willing to take a chance spilling words onto paper.
Use this discipline to increase my wisdom. Amen*

A Team Effort

The Egyptians became ruthless in imposing tasks on the Israelites.
—Exodus 1:13

Perhaps we're worried that we've become a little too proficient, a little too expert in the area of uncluttering and organizing our homes. Maybe we've seen signs that we're alienating those loved ones who live under the same roof. Or perhaps they're feeling left out. But do not despair, for there is an easy remedy. We simply decide what the next challenging organizational task might be and then call in the troops.

"It's time to clean the attic," you announce a few days before. "And I really need your help. But if we all do our parts, it might take only half a day." Then you assign specific tasks and offer some sort of tempting reward. And expect the usual complaints (unless you're living with polite aliens). But not only will you get your attic cleared out in record time, you will allow your family to enjoy the thrill of accomplishment as well.

SUCCESS STRATEGY

1. *Start with a specific list: Suzy sorts through old toys; Mom sifts through Granny's trunk; Timmy carries boxes up and down stairs; Dad fills pickup, takes to Goodwill . . .*
2. *Have necessary tools ready: boxes, trash bags, vacuum cleaner . . .*
3. *Offer a reward that the whole family can appreciate—pizza and putt-putt golf . . .*
4. *Dish out lots of praise and encouraging words—try to make it as fun as possible.*

PRAYER

Father, remind me that I'm not in this alone. Encourage me to include those around me and instill good habits in them as well.
Amen

Fail to Plan, Plan to Fail

Commit your work to the Lord, and your plans will be established.
—Proverbs 16:3

The hard fact is, clutterers, by nature, tend to be pretty poor planners. Even when we try to plan, our plans may become too extravagant or convoluted to succeed. So, maybe we need to learn a new way of planning. But first we must see the importance of planning. The bottom line is, if we don't plan, we immediately lose control of what happens next in our lives. For instance, when we go to the store without a list, we become victim to our own whims and the best sales tables.

So, even if we love spontaneity, we must begin to appreciate the balance a sensible and simple bit of planning can bring into our lives. And what we might not realize is that when we use a plan, like a blueprint, it allows us to create something bigger and better than we'd ever imagined.

A PLAN BOOK

This is a personal working notebook, different from a journal, that you keep in a handy place (kitchen, desk . . .) and where you jot down notes and ideas about things you'd like, or need, to do. Lists for grocery shopping. Chores that need doing. For instance, if Jenny wants a circus-themed birthday party next month, you might want to start jotting down some ideas, phone numbers, lists, etc. This book becomes an extension of your brain.

PRAYER

*Eternal God, help me to become a better planner—
not so I can increase the stress in my life,
but so I can better manage my time and energy. Amen*

Making the Most

Now there are varieties of gifts, but the same Spirit.
—1 Corinthians 12:4

We're all uniquely different, have different gifts, live in different regions, have different family situations. But, as recovering clutterers, we have some things in common. And the most obvious is our desire to move away from situations where we feel almost hopeless and into a new arena where it seems all things are possible. Well, almost. Naturally, we need to remember everyone has some limitations. And we sure don't want to slip back into the same trap of overloading ourselves again.

So let's consider who we are and what we have to work with, and then let's do the best with what we've got. Limited closet space? Well, let's see how innovative we can be with a trimmed-down wardrobe—think quality not quantity. Limited kitchen counter space? Let's think of new ways to get stuff off the counter. Hooks, shelves, perhaps a small butcher-block table with storage below? For where there's a problem, there must be a solution. Let's get creative and make the most of what we've got.

BATHROOM STORAGE-SHORTAGE IDEAS

1. *Consider keeping spare toilet-paper rolls in covered basket on top of toilet tank.*
2. *The wall above toilets is a great place for shelves to store bathroom extras.*
3. *How about a couple of small shelves near sink? Use decorative containers to hold things like extra soap, cotton balls, Q-Tips, etc.*
4. *Consider a stick-on shelf for the shower—they come in all shapes and sizes.*
5. *Consider hanging small shelves on the interior of vanity sink doors (for smaller items like shampoo, conditioner, lotion).*

PRAYER

Thank You, God, for life's little challenges. Teach me to think more creatively when it comes to problem solving. Amen

A God of Order

For everything there is a season,
and a time for every matter under heaven.
—Ecclesiastes 3:1

For those of us who grew out of cluttered roots, we could spend our lifetimes looking for the perfect replacement role model. But our search would be in vain, because we already have the perfect role model in Him who created the universe. Just look at the stars and planets, how they stay in perfect orbit and order. Or study the flowers that bloom and grow right on schedule. Or the animals that shed their thick coats before the heat of summer and get them back just in time for winter. God has designed creation to be incredibly orderly!

So when we need someone to learn from, someone to imitate, we need only look to God. Perhaps He's given us the seasons for just such a purpose. Maybe we can learn to simply tune in to God's rhythm of life and things like recycling and giving away will begin to make much more sense.

SEASONAL STUFF

1. *Spring is a great time to get rid of all those winter clothes you haven't worn in years (it saves you from having to store or dry-clean them).*
2. *Summer is good for those large cleaning-out projects (like garages, attics), when you need to cart things in and out.*
3. *Fall is the time to rid yourself of those worn-out sandals, tennis shoes, and clothes that really don't make you feel good. Toss them out instead of packing them away!*
4. *Winter is a good time for tedious organization tasks like putting photos in albums, labeling videocassettes, or creating a new filing system.*

PRAYER

Remind me, God, to take time to study the way You do things in nature. Thank You for being my perfect example. Amen

Listen to Your Heart

He woke up and rebuked the wind,
and said to the sea, "Peace! Be still!" Then the wind ceased,
and there was a dead calm.

—Mark 4:39

We live in such a noisy world—TVs, radios, video games, CD players, appliances, phones, you name it—and we sometimes forget how to listen for the really quiet things. How often we forget to settle down, enjoy the sounds of silence, and then listen to our own hearts. We fail to realize that noise is just another form of clutter. A cacophony of clutter. And something we'd all do well to escape from.

So, as we unclutter the visual world, why not consider the audio one as well? Why not create some silent spaces where we can sit alone and contemplate and meditate? How about some times where we can listen to the still, small voice of God, as well as the quiet, intuitive whispers of our own hearts? Who knows what we might hear.

UNCLUTTER THE AIR SPACE

1. *Next time you replace an appliance, consider getting the "quieter" one.*
2. *Try leaving TVs and radios off unless someone is specifically watching or listening to them.*
3. *Establish a quiet hour—perhaps in the early morning or after dinner—when all noise is banned.*
4. *Make "volume" rules for all forms of audio entertainment.*

PRAYER

Merciful Father, teach me to incorporate more quiet into my home and into my heart. Help me to tune in my ears to Your still, small voice. Amen

Small Setbacks

For this slight momentary affliction is preparing us for
an eternal weight of glory beyond all measure . . .
—2 Corinthians 4:17

It's inevitable that we'll have some setbacks and disappointments along the way in this life. This often seems to be the case the closer we get to reaching a particular goal. For example, you just clean out the spare room and turn it into some great storage space, as well as a delightful guest room, and suddenly your grown daughter decides she needs to come back home to live for a while.

So in order to preserve our sanity, we need to be able to go with the flow with some things. Occasionally, we just need to step back, take a deep breath, and pray for a better perspective. After all, our uncluttering goals aren't more important than human relationships. And in the long term, some things we view as distractions or disappointments might really be beautiful blessings in disguise.

ROOM FOR ONE MORE

What do you do if you're full up and your nephew drops in? Consider getting a self-inflating air mattress and keeping it with appropriate bed linens, pillow, and blanket in a large plastic bin. Perhaps tuck in a small "guest basket" as well (with towels, toiletries, a small alarm clock) and store until needed. Then you're ready for company on a moment's notice!

PRAYER

Dear God, help me to face the unexpected with an adventurous spirit, and to be graciously prepared for whatever comes my way.
Amen

Keeping It Simple

I have been paid in full and have more than enough.
—Philippians 4:18

We clutterers tend to overcomplicate life for ourselves and others. We, by nature, think more is better. And we take on too much. And as a result we unwittingly invite all sorts of stress into our lives. But if we could only learn to truly embrace simplicity and all that it stands for, our lives would probably run much more smoothly.

So, short of emblazoning a tattoo on our forehead, how can we imprint ourselves with a keep-it-simple mentality? Do we tape the message to our refrigerators, or write it in red lipstick on the bathroom mirror? How can we convince ourselves that simplicity is a truly good thing? Maybe seeing is believing. Maybe as we begin to practice simplicity in our day-to-day living, we will begin to see what a difference it makes.

KEEPING IT SIMPLE

1. *Simplify your shopping with a master list that's written in the order of the grocery store layout. Make copies of your list, then just check the items you need.*
2. *Simplify your morning routine by sporting a low-maintenance hairstyle.*
3. *Simplify the dinner hour by having a two-week rotating menu posted on the fridge.*
4. *Simplify social gatherings whenever possible. Make people, not activity, your focus.*

PRAYER

Almighty God, help me to value simplicity. Show me how to live and enjoy a life of simple abundance. Amen

Simple Pleasures

The Lord lift up his countenance upon you, and give you peace.
—Numbers 6:26

As we're working to wean ourselves from an unhealthy attachment to things, it's a good time to learn how to appreciate some of life's simpler pleasures. Because, as it turns out, simple pleasures are some of the most enjoyable pleasures in the world. We just get so distracted that we forget to take advantage of them. But now that we're uncluttering our lives a little, we might also be discovering we have more time.

We might have time for a quiet stroll around the neighborhood. Or time to read poetry or a good novel. We might have time (as well as an orderly enough kitchen) to try out a new recipe. Or time to simply sit quietly and hold hands with the one we love. We might even have time to run a delicious bubble bath and light candles. Or time to just sit in a rocking chair and enjoy the sensation of doing absolutely nothing at all!

SIMPLE PLEASURES 101

1. *It's okay to plan ahead for a simple pleasure.*
2. *Simple pleasures should be free (or very inexpensive).*
3. *Every day should have at least one simple pleasure.*
4. *You should never rush a simple pleasure.*
5. *Consider sharing a simple pleasure with someone you love.*

PRAYER

Dear Lord, help me to recognize my need for simple pleasures. Show me how to enjoy life more. Amen

It Might Come in Handy Someday

Now the Lord is the Spirit, and where the Spirit of the Lord is, there is freedom.

—2 Corinthians 3:17

Perhaps we're starting to imagine that we've become fairly free of our old cluttering ways. But let's not fool ourselves. Chances are we're still in the beginnings of this battle against clutter. For instance, let's open a seldom-used drawer and randomly pick out some items. Then let's ask ourselves these little questions: "Have I used this in the last year?" "Does it have any aesthetic or sentimental value to me?" If we answer no to both, then why do we hang on to it?

Ah, maybe we're thinking *but it might come in handy someday.* And what's the answer to *that* question? Of course, it might! *Anything* could come in handy under the right circumstances. A life-sized green elephant might come in handy for a child's birthday party, but does that mean we should keep one in the closet? Probably not.

FOR FURTHER REFLECTION

1. *Have you really pushed yourself far enough in the area of getting rid of stuff?*
2. *Why are you still clinging to things that only take up space?*
3. *Have you been asking those two questions and answering honestly?*
4. *What are you really afraid of losing by getting rid of things?*

PRAYER

Lord, I confess I might still be clinging to useless items that only bog me down. Please help me to realize the freedom I'll experience when I can let go. Amen

The Five Senses

They were astounded beyond measure,
saying, "He has done everything well; he even makes
the deaf to hear and the mute to speak."
—Mark 7:37

As clutterers, we may have learned to suppress our sensory perceptions. This could be the result of living amidst things we have trained our eyes not to see, sounds we have taught our ears to ignore, smells we simply don't notice, and so on. We may have forgotten how important our senses really are—and what a joy it is to experience pleasure. But as we chip away at the clutter in our homes, our senses can become more finely tuned and perceptive.

So now we can bring out some delightful elements (but not too many!) like scented candles, textured fabrics, pleasant colors, good music . . . and really give our senses a treat. And suddenly we'll be enjoying our homes and lives in a fresh, new way!

TUNE IN TO YOUR SENSES

Do you enjoy warm colors, unusual textures, and spicy smells, or do you prefer cooler tones, smooth textures, and clean scents? Do you like earth tones, homespun fabrics, and natural fragrances, or are you drawn to pastels, lace, and soothing lavender? Look at and smell and sample a variety of elements to determine your favorite delights and then incorporate them into your home.

PRAYER

Dear God, thank You for making me with the capacity to enjoy so many things. Help me to know myself better and to embrace my senses more fully. Amen

Celebrate Beauty

How lovely is your dwelling place,
O Lord of hosts!

—Psalm 84:1

Many clutterers can appreciate beauty, but are absolutely clueless about how to incorporate it into their daily lives. However, as the clutter is cleared away, we may discover a beauty in simplicity and order. And subsequently we may discover some new ways to introduce some touches of loveliness into our homes and lives. But we need to be careful not to go overboard: A little can go a long way.

One way to introduce beauty into your home is to find a decorative item or accent piece—like a painting, vase, or lamp—for a room you use a lot. Perhaps this is an item you already own but it's been buried beneath a pile of clutter. Bring it out, clean it up, and set it out. If you love it, let it usher in a new era of adding touches of beauty to your home. But go slowly. Play with it. Get to know your tastes before you indulge in an entire redecorating project.

SIMPLE STROKES OF BEAUTY

1. *Fresh flowers in a vase you love*
2. *A pretty silk scarf added to your wardrobe*
3. *An attractive accent pillow or colorful throw for the living room*
4. *A new tablecloth in a favorite color or pattern*

PRAYER

Thank You, Father, for the clean,
simple loveliness of the world
You made! Amen

An Orderly Reward

*He will transform the body of our humiliation
that it may be conformed to the body of his glory . . .*
—Philippians 3:21

Okay, now is the time to pull out those old "before" photos. And if you didn't take any, just try to remember how your home *used* to look. Have things gotten better? See any improvements yet? Hopefully we're starting to feel encouraged by now. Hopefully we can see a light at the end of the tunnel. And while we may still have some areas to conquer, some more mountains to climb (and remember we never quit contending against clutter), we can pause for a long moment and enjoy, even celebrate, how far we've come!

So, take some time to notice the difference. Take a deep breath and smile at how much better life feels now that you're getting control over stuff. Sure, maybe you can still see some problem areas, but try not to focus on those right now. Instead, just relax and thoroughly enjoy what you are creating. Give yourself some credit and relish your reward of a growing peace and orderliness.

WAYS TO ENJOY YOUR EFFORTS

1. *Make yourself a cup of tea (or whatever), sit down in your favorite area, and just soak in how things have changed.*
2. *Prepare a simple candlelit dinner to celebrate how far you've come.*
3. *Invite a couple of friends over for a simple, but fun evening.*

PRAYER

*Merciful Lord, help me to remember to take time
to appreciate what I'm working on. Thank You
for helping me to accomplish things in my life.
Amen*

Bite the Bullet

Those who conquer will inherit these things,
and I will be their God and they will be my children.
—Revelation 21:7

Chances are, we all have an overwhelming uncluttering task lurking ahead of us. Perhaps it's something we've been putting off, postponing until "just the right time." Most likely, it's intimidating or may even seem impossible. Maybe it's the garage, or a storage shed, or your mother's attic. But where do we begin? How will we ever finish? And what will we do with all that stuff? Maybe the time has come when we need to just bite the bullet, so to speak, and jump in.

The best way to fortify ourselves for this task is to begin thinking and speaking positively. Remind ourselves of those other challenging areas we have conquered. Tell ourselves how when we're done (and we will get done!) that we'll be so pleased and thrilled with our accomplishment that it will have been worth the effort. And, perhaps, even set up some sort of substantial reward.

TACKLING A MONSTER

1. *Start with a list or game plan, and estimate how long it will take.*
2. *Do you need to break this project into stages? Do you need help?*
3. *Plan this undertaking for when you're in your best "attack" mode.*
4. *Get your tools together, get on your best battle uniform, and charge!*

PRAYER

Almighty God, strengthen me as I prepare to take on
a big clutter challenge. Show me how to best go about this task.
And then give me the victory. Amen

The Upper Hand

So if you have been raised with Christ,
seek the things that are above, where Christ is,
seated at the right hand of God.

—Colossians 3:1

As we become more orderly and less cluttered, we focus less on surviving and more on actual living. We begin introducing elements of loveliness into our lives, and we enjoy our homes in whole new ways. In the past we were in the habit of reacting to our environment, but now we are becoming proactive. We are taking control and bringing our habitats into submission. And doesn't it feel great?

But another way we can get proactive is to start thinking ahead, planning forward. What expectations might we have of our homes? How can they serve us and our family better? What do we enjoy doing? What are our needs? How can we continue to organize our habitats in such a way that we'll not simply get by, but we'll function and perform at a whole new level?

ROOM FOR IMPROVEMENT

1. *How do you like to cook? Consider creating a "center" that makes your style of cooking easier (baking center, salad center, Asian cooking center).*
2. *Do you have a hobby? Consider creating an area (or even just a basket) that keeps everything right at your fingertips.*
3. *Where do you like to read? Is it a comfortable place equipped with a good reading light?*

PRAYER

Gracious God, thank You that life is for living.
Help me to seek out ways to live life more fully.
Amen

Realistic Goals

*Do not, therefore, abandon that confidence of yours; it brings a
great reward. For you need endurance, so that when you have done
the will of God, you may receive what was promised.*
—Hebrews 10:35, 36

It's possible the day may come, or has already arrived, when we
begin to feel so elated and delighted over a recent clutter victory
that we think we can do anything. And perhaps we can. But just
the same, we need to be realistic. We need to set attainable goals
and make sure we're in the habit of attaining them. As we progress,
we will be more prepared for greater challenges. And, who knows,
maybe someday we'll be helping others to escape from their
prisons of clutter.

In the meantime, let's continue to set realistic goals for
ourselves. Let's enjoy our successes and keep plugging along. Let's
keep pacing ourselves on a daily basis and maintain our self-
disciplines of regularly picking up, putting away, and throwing
out. And as new organization projects occur to us, let's list them
in our personal plan books, and then schedule in the times when
we think we can get to them.

WINDOW WASHING 101

1. *Collect your tools: a bucket, clean rags, a "professional" squeegee
   with extended handle, and a soft woolly "water applicator" head
   with extended handle.*
2. *Fill the bucket with about a gallon of warm water and a
   teaspoon of liquid dish soap.*
3. *Dip applicator tool in water, squeeze out excess, rub on window,
   then squeegee off.*
4. *Use rags to catch drips in corners.*

PRAYER

*Thank You, Lord, for helping me to increase my confidence.
Help me to stay on track. Amen*

Clear the Counters

Therefore I do my best always to have a clear conscience toward God and all people.

—Acts 24:16

One of the best ways to bring a kitchen back into order (especially after the onslaught of a teenage feeding frenzy) is to *clear the counters*. It's amazing how peace and order is instantly restored to a kitchen when those counters are clean and clear. It's like having a clean slate. And even if the floor needs sweeping, the dishwasher is full, and the refrigerator is empty, clean counters send the message that all is well. And sometimes that's a message we all need to hear.

But there may be ways we can clear those counters even more. Take a good look at your counters. What's on them? Only the items you use daily, like toaster and coffeemaker? Or do you still store other appliances there as well? Unless you have unlimited kitchen space, think of your countertops as prime real estate—put only what's really important there. And even then, there may be some ways to develop more space.

COUNTER EVALUATION

1. *Do you use what's on your counter daily?*
2. *Is it attractive to look at? (We need some things that please the eye.)*
3. *Is there another place or way it could be stored? Get creative.*

PRAYER

Dear God, help me to remember to clear the counters of life, too. Is there anyone I need to apologize to, or forgive? Help me to keep a clean slate. Amen

A Day Off

*Come to me, all you that are weary and are carrying heavy
burdens, and I will give you rest.*

—Matthew 11:28

We all need time off to refresh and recharge. Hopefully, none of
us have been waging our war on clutter 24/7. If so, it's time for a
break. And we need to give our families a break, too. However,
just because we're taking a "day off" doesn't mean we don't pick up
our dirty socks, neglect to make our beds, or allow the dishes to
pile up in the sink. Because how are we going to enjoy a day off if
we suddenly find ourselves surrounded by new piles of clutter?

No, even on a day off, we continue with our good, daily habits,
but we just don't take on any extra organization projects. Instead,
we allow ourselves time to regenerate and enjoy the company of
family and friends. We simply take it easy.

FOR FURTHER REFLECTION

1. *Do you feel compelled to accomplish something measurable every
   day?*
2. *Do people around you complain that you push them too hard?*
3. *Are you uncomfortable just doing nothing?*
4. *Do you take time for just plain fun?*

PRAYER

*Heavenly Father, help me to remember
how You rested after creating the world.
Show me how I can enjoy a day of rest, too. Amen*

Comfort Drawer

Call to me and I will answer you, and will tell you great and hidden things that you have not known.

—Jeremiah 33:3

Okay, now that we've cleared things out, we should have more space. Right? Perhaps it's time to think about creating a "comfort drawer." But what is a comfort drawer, you ask? Well, there come times when, for one reason or another, we could use a little extra bit of comfort. And at such times, we often find it's up to us to provide the goodies ourselves.

So, look for a spare drawer (preferably in your bedroom) and begin to fill it with some "little treasures" that you will allow yourself to be pampered with in a time of need. Perhaps you'll include a special bath oil, a really good book, a fuzzy pair of socks, a comforting nightie, a scented candle, a special herbal tea, or even a favorite chocolate treat. When the time comes, your comfort drawer will be there just waiting for you.

CREATURE COMFORTS

1. *A soft, fluffy throw to curl up in*
2. *A pair of fuzzy slippers*
3. *A blank book for journaling*
4. *A deliciously scented hand lotion*

PRAYER

Lord, help me to remember to nurture myself, especially when I'm running on empty. And remind me to turn to You for love and encouragement. Amen

Keeping Vigil

I long for your salvation, O Lord,
and your law is my delight.

—Psalm 119:174

Okay, maybe we're so highly evolved in this area of clutter recovery that we really don't need this reminder anymore. But just in case . . . let's all take a moment to poke around our homes, our workplaces, our yards. Now, what do we see? Is everything we're finding (including stuff tucked way in the backs of our closets and drawers) *useful or attractive or sentimentally important?* Let's be honest. Have we really arrived yet?

So, perhaps we need to ask ourselves once again—why are we keeping this? If it doesn't meet our "keeper" criteria, why haven't we given it away or thrown it out yet?

PRECIOUS PIECES

1. *Always treat your child's artwork and schoolwork as prized possessions (not clutter!).*
2. *Display current pieces prominently—on the refrigerator or in a "slip-in" box frame that's hung for all to see (and replace with new work regularly).*
3. *Use a large art portfolio or box (one per child) for storing these treasures away. If it becomes too full, consider going through it with your child and picking several pieces to keep each year. Or get another portfolio.*

PRAYER

Eternal God, thank You for the progress I've made.
Help me to keep growing in the area of organization,
and help me to learn to really see what's around me. Amen

Dream a Little Dream

*. . . your sons and your daughters shall prophesy, your old men
shall dream dreams, and your young men shall see visions.*

—Joel 2:28

Maybe we used to dream of living or working in a place where
chaos and clutter no longer ruled, a pleasant habitat where peace
and order and serenity reigned supreme. But perhaps we now find
ourselves much closer to, or even *actually living* that fantasy in real
life. And if that's the case, if we've attained one dream, maybe it's
time to start dreaming another.

For how is it that dreams come to us? Don't they often occur
while we're content and relaxed? Sitting back and putting our
feet up? Like those times we allow ourselves the luxury of
imagining beyond, thinking bigger, hoping for better. Isn't that
what dreams are made of? For that's when we have the confidence
that we can go after something more, that we can attain something
slightly impossible. For we believe if we apply some hard work, a
better focus, receive a little grace . . . then perhaps our dreams *will*
come true.

THE STUFF OF DREAMS

1. *Allow yourself the time and luxury to dream.*
2. *Ask yourself what you really want in life.*
3. *Ask yourself what steps you might take to get there.*
4. *Begin to implement the first steps.*

PRAYER

*Dear God, teach me to be a dreamer. Give me the faith
I need to dream the kind of dreams that would bring
true fulfillment to my life. Amen*

Entertaining Thoughts

The Lord is gracious and merciful, slow to anger and abounding in steadfast love. The Lord is good to all, and his compassion is over all that he has made.

—Psalm 145:8, 9

It's possible that after so many years of feeling buried in clutter we may be out of the habit of entertaining. After all, who cared to have friends over for dinner when they couldn't even find the stove? But times are changing and we are, too. And maybe we're starting to realize how fulfilling it is to enjoy our homes, and maybe we'd like to share them with others, too. But where do we begin?

First of all, let's start small—remember those baby steps? We don't have to start with a seven-course meal for a party of twelve. We can invite a neighbor over for coffee or tea. We can have a couple over for dessert. Or maybe just popcorn and a movie. The important thing is to open our doors, and start enjoying the company of family and friends. And our goal is to make them comfortable and at home. Then everyone, including us, has a good time!

HOSPITALITY PREPAREDNESS

1. *Always have a foolproof dinner trick up your sleeve (something you can pull together from your pantry or freezer on a moment's notice).*
2. *Keep your hot beverage supply stocked up (a basket containing gourmet coffees, cocoas, teas, cider mixes).*
3. *Hide away some pretty paper napkins and candles for instant and easy festivity.*

PRAYER

Gracious Lord, teach me how to make people feel welcome and comfortable in my home. Amen

Great Preparations

The house that I am about to build will be great,
for our God is greater than other gods.
—2 Chronicles 2:5

Being prepared must be one of the biggest keys to success—in any area. Consider old Noah and how long it must have taken him to prepare for the Zoo Cruise. Can you imagine his shopping list? But good preparedness doesn't just mean having all the right stuff to pull something off. It also means having things in the right places so we can work efficiently. Imagine how frustrating it would have been for Noah if the lion food had been buried way down beneath the hyena food—and guess what the lions would have been eating instead.

And so, as we consider events we need to prepare for—special times like a surprise birthday party or a Christmas dinner or a graduation celebration, or even ordinary things like tonight's dinner—we cannot underestimate the value of having a place for everything and everything in its place. And that's how we're truly prepared.

AN OUNCE OF PREPARATION

1. *The best preparations begin with list making and calendar checking.*
2. *If you're planning something huge (like a wedding) you may want to start from the big date and work backward to see how much time you'll really need for each element.*
3. *Remember your gift log? Consider adding a section for entertaining—it can help you stock up and plan ahead.*
4. *Consider having an "entertaining" cupboard for party supplies, punch bowls, large serving dishes, etc. If you don't entertain frequently it can be away from the kitchen.*

PRAYER

Loving Father, teach me to be prepared for what's coming my way.
Help me to be a better planner. Amen

A Time and Place

Therefore my heart is glad, and my soul rejoices;
my body also rests secure.

—Psalm 16:9

Sometimes the pure busyness of life teaches us to ignore our inner clocks. For instance, if a certain work project must be completed by five, we simply do it, even if we're running low on mental juices and suspect it's not our best work. But as we learn to better pace ourselves, we might also learn to tune in to how, where, and why we perform better. We might even come up with ways to utilize our peak performance times better.

Some of us might do best in midmorning, working at a quiet desk, while others might peak in the evening, surrounded by noise and activity. But when we understand what works for us, we're wise to employ strategies that allow us to function most effectively. It may mean hiring a sitter so we can write a sharper proposal. It could mean locating our desk away from distractions. But we're the only ones who can figure ourselves out.

THE WAY WE WORK

1. *Schedule mindless, cleanup activities during times when your mind is weary.*
2. *Plan "high performance" activities when you know you're at your peak.*
3. *Take a power nap (ten to twenty minutes) as needed to clear and refresh your mind.*
4. *Avoid too many carbohydrates for lunch (they make you sleepy).*
5. *Use light exercise to get your mind and body energized.*

PRAYER

Lord God, show me how to tune in to my body and inner clock better. Help me to recognize when I need rest or exercise. Amen

Creative Alternatives

*So if anyone is in Christ, there is a new creation: everything old
has passed away; see, everything has become new!*
—2 Corinthians 5:17

Everyone has some unique clutter problems to resolve. And this is
an area where creativity can play a wonderful role. In fact, the
more we utilize our creative resources the more we appreciate it
when new challenges (no longer called problems) arise. For
instance, what do you do with all those umbrellas and boots and
coats that tend to pile up by your back door? Maybe you employ
that old wooden toy box (no longer in use) as a bench to store
boots and umbrellas, and then hang a set of hefty wooden coat
hooks above. And now you have a great area for people to sit down
and remove their boots and hang their coats.

But for those who have trouble getting their creative juices
flowing, just look in the self-help/organizational section of the
library and you're sure to find advice for almost any challenge you
can think up.

CREATIVE USES FOR A FISHING TACKLE BOX

1. *Storing cosmetics or manicure supplies*
2. *Organizing and storing jewelry*
3. *Sorting and storing small craft supplies*
4. *Storing cake decorating supplies*

PRAYER

*Thank You, Lord, for creating me in Your own creative image.
Help me to develop and use my own creativity. Amen*

Happy Talk

For they will scarcely brood over the days of their lives,
because God keeps them occupied with the joy of their hearts.
—Ecclesiastes 5:20

If we have spent years as clutterers, it's quite likely we may have some negative image problems dogging at our heels. It's possible that we have acquired the habit of mentally berating or accusing ourselves of things like laziness, carelessness, and foolishness.

Have you ever seen a church bell that someone's been ringing? Do you remember how the bell continued to ring long after the person let go of the rope? That's how it can be with us. Even if we quit saying those negative words about ourselves, we may still be hearing them inside. And that's why we need to start using "happy talk." We need to start telling ourselves positive things—even if it feels a little silly at first. Like, "Great job straightening that drawer." Or, "You're such a good organizer!" Or, "What nice work you did in the kitchen tonight! Julia Child would be proud of you!"

LEARN THE WORDS

1. *Begin to mentally affirm yourself, your work, your value, your intelligence.*
2. *Make a point to verbally affirm those around you on a regular basis.*
3. *Make a list of all the things you do really well.*
4. *Praise God for all He's done and is doing in your life.*

PRAYER

God, teach me to think and speak more positively about myself as well as others. Thank You and praise You for the work You're doing within me. Amen

True Inspiration

O Lord, in the morning you hear my voice;
in the morning I plead my case to you, and watch.
—Psalm 5:3

In our organizational efforts, as in our lives, we will continue to have areas of weakness, places where we could use some improvement, a little tweaking here and there. Maybe it's in revamping an office space. Perhaps it's getting our kitchens in top functioning order. Or it could be our wardrobes, or our decorating attempts. Or maybe it's in our relationships and our behavior. But sometimes we just lose steam. No matter what the issue—personal, professional, or simply systematic—God is the One to turn to.

God has a plan for us. He alone knows what we need, what we should be focused on, what we should be accomplishing and concerned about. If we turn to Him when we are perplexed, the way will be made plain to us. Big-ticket items, little-ticket items—He's there to direct us.

FOR FURTHER REFLECTION

If you tend to think prayer should be reserved for "weighty" issues, have you ever noticed how heavy the seemingly lightweight things become when you carry them all by yourself? Remember that God is available to help you every day in every way.

PRAYER

Almighty God, show me the areas of my life that could use some improvement. Give me the wisdom to seek Your guidance in all things. Amen

Kitchen Harmony

I will make them and the region around my hill a blessing;
and I will send down the showers in their season;
they shall be showers of blessing.

—Ezekiel 34:26

Probably the most used room in the American home is the kitchen. And it has the potential to contain the most chaos and clutter. But assuming we've reduced the clutter by now, let's look at some ways to make our kitchens more efficient. Because all kitchens and families are different, you can begin by studying how your kitchen is used. Look at the traffic patterns. Where are the pileups located? Then consider ways to reroute.

For instance, are your dish cabinets close to the dishwasher? Or are they on the other end of the room? Are your pans near the stove? Baking supplies near the counters and the oven? Table linens near the dining area? Think about where and why you store things where you do. Can it be done more efficiently?

MAKESHIFT PANTRIES

1. *Use a baker's rack with clever containers for dry goods and baskets for fresh produce.*
2. *Find a freestanding wardrobe and install shelves.*
3. *A narrow but tall bookshelf can provide pantry space in a kitchen corner.*
4. *Even a small broom closet can be an effective pantry when outfitted with shelves (you can probably keep the brooms and mops in the laundry room instead).*

PRAYER

Merciful Father, help me to create a kitchen that is as warm and welcoming as it is efficient. And bless the times spent there.
Amen

Kitchen Control

See, I made him a witness to the peoples,
a leader and commander for the peoples.
—Isaiah 55:4

As with finances, the kitchen fares far better with one captain at the helm. This doesn't mean that everyone can't share this communal space, but to keep things running smoothly and efficiently, one person needs to take the lead—especially when it comes to establishing where things go. But if we're smart we'll try to create a very user-friendly system, something that makes sense to everyone and is easy to maintain.

Unfortunately this can't always be accomplished overnight—it tends to be a trial and error process. But the key here is to pay attention to what works and what doesn't and then fix it so it works. For instance, if someone in your family loves making salads, then establish an area (near the sink) where they can have everything handy, and where they can work undisturbed.

ORGANIZING RECIPES

1. *Use an expanding file folder to hold loose recipes you want to try (label each section appropriately—desserts, main dishes, breads).*
2. *After trying a recipe (and liking it) upgrade it to a three-ring magnetic photo album (also arranged by section). The plastic sheet on the page will protect the recipe while you cook.*
3. *To save time with cookbooks, list the page numbers of your favorite recipes inside the front cover.*

PRAYER

Lord, help me to make my kitchen fun, functional,
and a place where everyone feels at home. Amen

Refrigerator Elbow

Day by day, as they spent much time together in the temple,
they broke bread at home and ate their food with
glad and generous hearts . . .

—Acts 2:46

Which door in your kitchen gets opened more times a day than any other? Chances are it's the refrigerator's. The fridge is probably the hub of the kitchen. And if your kitchen is smartly designed, your refrigerator will be in one point of a triangle that connects with your sink and stove. But there are some tricks to keeping your refrigerator less cluttered and easier to use.

Group "like" items together and use specific areas for certain foods (so people aren't always hunting for something). Put cheeses and lunch meats together; keep milk and juices on the same shelf; store eggs and other breakfast items together. Have a designated and prominent spot for leftovers where people can get to them easily, and where they won't get shoved to the back. Store seldom-used items like pickled turnips in the rear in those harder-to-reach spots.

FREEZER TIPS

1. *Use colored freezer bags to easily recognize foods (yellow for poultry, red for meat, green for produce).*
2. *Mark and date everything (use Velcro to adhere freezer marker to freezer).*
3. *Place new items in back, move older items forward.*
4. *Use a freezer "blueprint" to show where items go (meat to left, bread in center, juice on right) to avoid the constant digging-for-treasure syndrome.*

PRAYER

Help me, God, to be a good steward of money in the way
I purchase and maintain the food in my home. Amen

Take a Break

Restore us, O Lord God of hosts; let your face shine,
that we may be saved.

—Psalm 80:19

Perhaps it's time to consider one of those rewards that you've been promising yourself (you know, for all those tasks you've been tackling recently). Or maybe all you need is a really good break. In fact, when was the last time you took a real break? Chances are, if you work in the home or for yourself, you could be long overdue. Because, the truth is, we tend to be pretty hard taskmasters. Especially when we're consumed with a new idea like reorganizing our space. And sometimes we might forget to tell ourselves to go and take a break. And we all know what they say about all work and no play.

So, maybe we need to start scheduling in our break time. And then make sure we're taking it. Our minds and bodies need time to relax and regenerate. Then, when we return to our tasks, we're that much better equipped to continue.

BREAK TIPS

1. *Try to take your breaks at consistent times each day.*
2. *Don't automatically use caffeine or carbohydrates as your "pick-me-ups."*
3. *Consider using a break time for a daily walk.*
4. *Enjoy the company of others during your break (but if it's on the phone, make sure you're giving your body a break from its normal working position).*

PRAYER

Dear God, thank You for work and rest.
Show me how to balance these elements in my life. Amen

New Ideas

Teach me, and I will be silent;
make me understand how I have gone wrong.

—Job 6:24

As we progress in organizing and streamlining our homes and work spaces, we'll naturally be attuned to new ideas. They pop up in newspapers and periodicals, on TV shows and online, and even around the company watercooler. But it's not always easy or practical to immediately implement every new idea. So, perhaps we need to get in the habit of jotting them down in our plan book (in a "future projects" section). Or maybe we'll want to create a special file folder to contain notes and magazine clippings about helpful ideas and potential projects.

But an openness to new ideas is healthy. In fact, our lives and homes could be compared to a pool of water. To remain vital and wholesome we need fresh water to come in and stale water to go out. So let's stay open and receptive to new organizing ideas. And let's be willing to let go of ideas that aren't working so well.

IDEA SOURCES

1. *Books on organization*
2. *Online resources*
3. *Lifestyle section of newspaper*
4. *Home-oriented magazines*
5. *Home-focused TV shows*

PRAYER

Help me, Lord, to continue to embrace learning.
I don't want to become stuck in old and inefficient ways.
Breathe Your creativity into me. Amen

Charitable Gifts

Every generous act of giving, with every perfect gift,
is from above, coming down from the Father of lights,
with whom there is no variation or shadow due to change.
—James 1:17

Hopefully, by now we've become familiar with some of the charitable thrift shops in our neighborhood. Perhaps we've established a favorite organization, and maybe they even know us by name, or smile when they see us coming. And, if that's the case, we've probably experienced the thrill that comes with giving—and giving generously!

It's interesting that as these relationships develop (especially as we begin to more fully understand the ways some of these organizations reach out to the homeless and helpless) we start to feel a partnership with them. And we may find that we want to donate even more. Perhaps we'll become even more ruthless in our uncluttering. Or maybe we'll roll up our sleeves and volunteer a chunk of our time. But the fact is, giving to others changes us. It changes our thinking, our habits, our attitudes . . . and it transforms us into more caring and generous people.

BE PREPARED TO GIVE

1. *Keep the phone number and hours of your favorite charity thrift shops handy.*
2. *Schedule a regular monthly pickup from your home with those organizations that provide collection services.*
3. *Consider inquiring about volunteer opportunities with charitable groups.*

PRAYER

Gracious Lord, thank You for giving so much to me.
Help me to continue the flow of giving to others.
Bless them through me. Amen

Closet Control

Your way was through the sea, your path,
through the mighty waters; yet your footprints were unseen.
—Psalm 77:19

What space in our homes is most likely to become disorganized and cluttered faster than any other? If we're like most people, it's our closets. And the reason for this is probably twofold: 1) because closets wind up holding everything we can't find room for anywhere else, and 2) because it's easy to think of them as *hiding* places. But unfortunately, ignoring the condition of our closets only serves to add to the chaos in our lives.

So, in addition to reducing our closet clutter, what can we do to improve things? Perhaps we need to invest in some closet organizing tools. Hooks, shelves, special hangers, boxes, and storage bags are all readily available in most hardware stores or home centers. And for those ready to make the big commitment, there are businesses (look in the yellow pages) that specialize in closet organization.

STRAIGHTENING THINGS OUT

1. *Try to pinpoint your closets' trouble spots (not enough shelves, not enough rod space, shoes all over the floor, accessories hard to find, things that should be in separate closets thrown together in one).*
2. *Take measurements and make notes. Consider rearranging a wall for two levels of rods; or hanging accessory hooks, a shoe bag, or a tool board; or making room for stacked shelves or crates.*
3. *Take your notes to a home center. Ask about their return policy. Perhaps you can take home several options and see what works best, then return the others.*

PRAYER

Loving Father, remind me that "unseen" elements
play a vital role in living. Amen

Always on Our Toes

Keep alert, stand firm in your faith, be courageous, be strong.
—1 Corinthians 16:13

No matter where we are—kitchen, bathroom, bedroom, or garage—we need to remember to continue to scrutinize how often we use the things around us. If we haven't used a particular item in the last year, chances are we don't need it and it's just taking up valuable space. Of course there are exceptions to this, including things that have significant sentimental value (like wedding gowns, heirlooms, photos, particularly memorable baby clothes), but when it comes to plain old ordinary *stuff* that's just sitting around collecting dust, we can never let our guard down.

We must always keep on our toes, clearing out on a regular basis. But hopefully, we've already discovered the joy of getting rid of what we don't need or use.

MEDICINE CABINET TIPS

1. *Always keep secure with safety latches if small children are about.*
2. *Store frequently used items (toothpaste, floss, mouthwash) on lower shelf.*
3. *Keep over-the-counter items together (cold medicines, pain relievers).*
4. *Place prescription medications on highest shelf (dispose of expired medications).*
5. *Keep well-equipped first-aid kit near kitchen or bathroom (or any other water source).*
6. *Post first-aid instructions and location of first-aid kit inside cabinet door.*

PRAYER

Thank You, God, for bringing me so far.
Help me to keep moving forward. Amen

The Friendly Box

Those who love a pure heart and are gracious in speech
will have the king as a friend.

—Proverbs 22:11

As we become more adept at clutter removal, we may become known for our generous ways. Who'd have thought? But by now, your young niece might fondly remember how you gave her your fringed-leather coat from the '70s. Or a neighbor may be eternally grateful for that fondue pot. And we might be discovering how fun it is to give away things we no longer need or use to others who thoroughly appreciate them.

For that reason, we might consider creating a "friendly box." This is a special box (we might keep it by the front door or in the coat closet) where we place nice items that we are now ready to get rid of—items that someone dear to us might truly enjoy. Then when friends or family are over, we can invite them to take their pick from the box. And then just watch as eyes light up—it's like a year-round Christmas!

YOUR FRIENDLY BOX

1. *Chose an attractive box or basket if you'll be keeping this by the front door—you don't need an eyesore there.*
2. *Consider tagging certain items for certain people.*
3. *Commit yourself to emptying the box regularly (sending leftover items to charity).*

PRAYER

Dear Lord, thank You for showing me how much fun
it is to be generous. Please increase my ability
to give cheerfully to others. Amen

Back to the Laundry Room

*You blind Pharisee! First clean the inside of the cup,
so that the outside also may become clean.*
—Matthew 23:26

Now that we've uncluttered our laundry rooms, it's time to streamline our lives some more (and save time) by learning a few new laundry room tricks. Consider color-coding things like hangers, laundry baskets, sheets, towels (for each family member or room) to make for simpler sorting. Try using nylon mesh bags for delicate items (on gentle cycle) to reduce the number of things you have to wash by hand.

Utilize your hangers and rods to eliminate or reduce the need to iron. Remove knit clothes promptly from dryer, thoroughly shake and hang while still warm for virtually wrinkle-free clothes. Keep your washer and dryer clean by dipping a paper towel into soapy water and giving the machines a quick wipe-down after every load. And don't forget to remove the lint from your dryer after every load, too—it should improve the performance of the machine, perhaps reducing drying time.

LAUNDRY TIPS

1. *For cleaner laundry, run water and soap for a couple of minutes before adding clothes.*
2. *Provide family with safety pins to keep socks together while laundering.*
3. *Label designated areas (or baskets) for each family member's clean laundry (they can pick it up themselves).*
4. *Recycle used static-free dryer sheets to clean TV screens and computer monitors.*

PRAYER

*God, thank You for both spiritual and physical cleanliness.
I know I take such things for granted, but remind me
what a gift being clean is! Amen*

Quick Cleanups

But those who are noble plan noble things,
and by noble things they stand.

—Isaiah 32:8

Although we accept it as a necessary part of living, most of us don't particularly enjoy spending too much time housecleaning. And we're usually grateful for any new ways to streamline the process. One way to save steps is to store cleaning items near the areas we use them. Instead of keeping all our cleaning items beneath the sink or in the laundry room, we might consider some other options. For instance, we might keep furniture polish and a dust rag in a drawer in the living room or dining room (where most of our wood furnishings are kept).

We might want to keep a mini-vacuum near a stairway for quick use. Or perhaps we'll outfit a small plastic container with shower-scrubbing supplies and park it in a corner of the shower (to encourage other users to pitch in). Also, in a two-story home, we'll save a lot of lugging by having both an upstairs and downstairs vacuum, as well as a full set of appropriate cleaning supplies for each level.

ALTERNATIVE CLEANING TOOLS

1. *An old toothbrush works wonders cleaning grout.*
2. *A trim-size paintbrush is wonderful for cleaning mini-blinds.*
3. *Q-Tips dipped in furniture polish are a great way to reach tightly carved spots.*
4. *Old nylons with furniture polish can buff wood surfaces smooth.*

PRAYER

Thank You, Lord, for my home. Thank You for teaching me
to be a good steward of all You've blessed me with
(including my time!). Amen

Living Free

For freedom Christ has set us free.
Stand firm, therefore, and do not submit again
to a yoke of slavery.

—Galatians 5:1

Isn't it great—*finally*—to be enjoying all our "inalienable" rights: life, liberty, and the pursuit of happiness? And because we can really appreciate our new freedom from the bondage of clutter, we'll be more likely to continue in the patterns we've worked so hard to establish. Because the fact is, our new freedom (like all freedoms) was purchased at a price. We spent a fair amount of sweat, and maybe even tears, to get here.

Let's not forget how life used to be when we existed in a prison (of our own making, of course) where the confining walls were erected from mountains of clutter and too much stuff. A place where stressful complications were the norm, and we felt certain there was no escape. But now we're free! And let's continue to live free, valuing our space and peace, and having a place for everything. Let's celebrate our freedom!

BATHROOM TRICKS

1. *Install a paper-towel holder on the inside of the vanity cupboard door (for quick cleanups).*
2. *Use a paper-cup dispenser (for sanitation and ease).*
3. *When cool, stash curling iron and blow-dryer in an attractive basket, along with brushes and such.*
4. *Use eye-catching containers to organize makeup. Tubular items are easy to identify in mugs or glasses. Metal boxes with lids work well for other cosmetics.*

PRAYER

Father in Heaven, thank You for the new freedom
I'm experiencing in my life. Amen

Spread the Joy

Do not lag in zeal, be ardent in spirit, serve the Lord.
—Romans 12:11

When we're really excited about something, it's hard to keep our happiness from bubbling over onto everyone around us. But just the same, we want to be careful in how we go about sharing our enthusiasm. Just as a smoker doesn't appreciate being lectured by a recovering smoker on the best methods of quitting, so other clutterers might resent our zeal in telling them how easily they, too, can shape up their lives.

But there are some less intimidating ways we can encourage others, especially those who are aware of our former cluttering habits. For one thing, we might invite them into our home—just for a nice social visit. Remember, a picture's worth a thousand words. And, if they're impressed, they'll probably ask us how we did it. And when we do talk about our success, it's important to humbly remember we used to be just like them (maybe even worse!).

BEDTIME COMFORTS

1. *Create a place near your bed (basket, drawer, bag on a hook) to contain those things you like to use there (TV remote, reading glasses, nail file, notepad).*
2. *Consider a bed tray or table (if you enjoy eating or drinking in bed).*
3. *Do you read in bed? How about a nice bolster pillow to support your back or neck?*
4. *If you sit in bed (to watch TV or read) a soft afghan can warm up cool shoulders.*

PRAYER

*Lord God, thank You for Your kind and loving grace in my life.
Help me to display that same sort of compassion and empathy
for those around me. Amen*

Price of Peace

. . . serve him with single mind and willing heart;
for the Lord searches every mind, and understands
every plan and thought.

—1 Chronicles 28:9

What is the value of peace? Can we even put a price tag on it? And yet, it's never free, is it? Like our freedom, it's been purchased at a price—a high price! In fact, many of us had to actually "go to war" for it. We had to roll up our sleeves and fight the battle against stuff and clutter. We had to remain diligent against all odds, and we had to refuse to surrender. But, despite all that effort, when we consider the reward, hasn't it all been worth the struggle?

On some levels, we may have to continue this battle for peace. For surely, there are new contenders that come at us regularly, trying to steal our peace away. Whether it's nuisance phone calls, blocked plumbing, or an impossible deadline, we can expect these interruptions to continue. Perhaps that's why it's so important to maintain our inner peace. For that sort of peace, within ourselves and with God, is not easily disturbed by outward circumstances and can sustain us through life's tougher challenges.

A PIECE OF PEACE

1. *Take a moment to breathe deeply.*
2. *Quiet your heart before God.*
3. *Thank God for His goodness and mercy in your life.*
4. *Entrust God with your daily concerns.*

PRAYER

Eternal God, help me to get a grasp on the exterior turmoil
in my life, and help me to come to You on a daily basis
for my inner peace. Amen

Hyacinth for the Soul

And all who have this hope in him purify themselves,
just as he is pure.

—1 John 3:18

In our quest for organization and order, we want to guard against creating an environment that feels totally barren or sterile. It's possible things might seem a little stark, as we strip away clutter that really has no importance to us. It's possible we could be left with some bare floors and empty spaces. But even that can be compared to the purity of a blank canvas that's just waiting for someone to place a stroke of color here, a contour there . . .

So if our habitats are feeling slightly sparse, let's not rush out trying to immediately and haphazardly fill those spaces again. Instead, let's learn, from our Japanese neighbors, the art of minimalism—the beauty of simplicity. And let's find a "hyacinth for our soul"—that one exquisitely beautiful thing that will touch us and guide us to beauty.

HOW TO FIND A "HYACINTH"

1. *Once again, get in touch with your likes and dislikes.*
2. *You might start by looking through interior design magazines—tear out some scenes that appeal to you—maybe circle a particular item (lamp, rug, table, painting).*
3. *Ask yourself what it is that most appeals to you about it (item, color, style?).*
4. *Make a list and begin to look for just the right piece. Depending on your budget, you can try a secondhand store, craft shop, import store, or an interior design shop.*
5. *Don't settle for less than what you really love.*

PRAYER

God, my Creator, help me to appreciate beauty,
and to understand it's as unique as I am. Teach me
to know myself and my personal tastes better. Amen

A Nurturing Place

One thing I asked of the Lord, that will I seek after:
to live in the house of the Lord all the days of my life,
to behold the beauty of the Lord, and to inquire in his temple.
—Psalm 27:4

They say our homes should reflect who we are. Some are flamboyant and colorful, while others are quiet and subdued. Some are eclectic and flow with creativity, and some are tailored and modern. And isn't it great that there's so much diversity to be enjoyed? But perhaps there's something our homes might have in common. For who among us wouldn't desire that our habitat be a nurturing place?

It's not uncommon for us to come home in search of solace, comfort, and nurturing; how precious it is when we find it! And so as we begin to discover and build upon what we believe is the character of our home (indeed a reflection of ourselves), let's keep nurturing in mind. Let's create a haven where we can safely gather and leave feeling encouraged. What could be better than that?

NURTURING THE SENSES

1. *Warm color tones (gold, russets, naturals, wood tones) make us feel welcome.*
2. *Some scented candles (vanilla, spice, cocoa) feel warm and nurturing.*
3. *Soft textures (velvet, fur, chenille) suggest comfort.*
4. *Certain styles of music soothe, uplift, inspire, encourage.*
5. *Hot drinks (cocoa, tea, coffee, warm milk) are soothing.*

PRAYER

Lord, You are my haven. I love that I can come to You
for healing and love and encouragement. Let my home
be like that for others. Amen

Never Done

Beware, keep alert; for you do not know
when the time will come.

—Mark 13:33

Part of the fun and challenge of our war on clutter is that we'll never be finished. Because, as we've already noticed, clutter and stuff just keeps coming at us. Whether it's from Christmas or the passing of a beloved elderly aunt, we're sure to be continually deciding what stays and what goes. But once again we can rely on that old pool metaphor—in with the good and out with the bad. So we will continually sift and sort.

But the good news is, it gets so much easier with time. It's likely the day will come when it's second nature, and we don't even notice we're doing it. Just as the trees shed their leaves every fall, we'll be sending off a box to Goodwill. And as the trees get new leaves in the spring, we may be bringing home a beautiful green afghan to throw on the back of the sofa.

SOME DESKTOP TIPS

1. *A knickknack shelf makes for additional storage space for small desk items.*
2. *That one lone coffee mug is great for holding pens and pencils.*
3. *Small inexpensive plastic containers are great for storing loose supplies.*
4. *Divided wall organizers (for papers and files) free up valuable desk space.*
5. *A picnic basket is perfect for storing extra packs of paper, envelopes, and bulky items.*

PRAYER

Dear God, remind me that most things in life are continual.
Help me to be thankful for each new task, just as I am thankful
for each new day. Amen

Earth Friendly

And God said, "Let the waters bring forth
swarms of living creatures, and let birds fly above the earth
across the dome of the sky."

—Genesis 1:20

Now that we have our homes under control (or almost) perhaps it's time to become a little more environmentally conscious and ask ourselves if we're doing all we can to be "earth friendly." Do we maintain separate bins for our recyclable items (like glass, metal, plastic)? Are we boxing our newspapers and magazines? Do we save our wet garbage for the compost pile? And if not, why not?

Recycling is a great chore for children. After all, they'll be inhabiting the planet longer than us, so they might as well start caring for it now. But in order for them to be successful, we need to set up systems that work. We need to make sure they have what they need, where they need it, so they can do the job right. And then, as always, we need to reward them with our sincere praise and gratitude.

RECYCLING TOOLS

1. *Clearly labeled bins (consider color coding: green/glass, blue/metal, yellow/plastic)*
2. *Paper-towel holder, with paper towels (for cleanups)*
3. *Crates or boxes for newspapers and magazines*
4. *Small plastic bucket (near kitchen sink) for wet garbage to go to compost*

PRAYER

Loving Father, thank You for this beautiful world you've made!
Help me to live responsibly in it and to teach my family
to do likewise. Amen

Simplify, Simplify, Simplify

But strive first for the kingdom of God and his righteousness,
and all these things will be given to you as well.
—Matthew 6:33

There probably isn't a single area in our lives that wouldn't improve with just a little bit of simplification. Whether it's our homes, our workplaces, our daily commute, or even our relationships, simplicity almost always makes things smoother and better. And yet, it seems everything within our modern day culture fights against this. It seems we're constantly bombarded by subtle messages that suggest that by complicating our lives we'll be much happier.

So, if we're ever to fully understand the wonders of simplicity, we may need to teach ourselves a few things. We might have to say "No, thank you" more often. Or skip that big clearance sale. We may need to slow down instead of speeding up. And we need to remember it's the simple things in life that mean the most—things like love and laughter and family and friends. And then maybe we'll get it right.

SOME SIMPLE SOLUTIONS

1. *Need more space?—give something away.*
2. *Need more time?—give something up.*
3. *Need more love?—give some away.*

PRAYER

Dear Lord, I confess I sometimes forget to slow down
and live more simply. Please help me to understand and appreciate
the benefits of simplicity. Amen

What Really Matters

I give you a new commandment, that you love one another.
Just as I have loved you, you also should love one another.

—John 13:34

Suppose we've got our homes totally uncluttered, perfectly organized, and things are looking pretty good. And we're feeling pretty good, too. But perhaps we need to pause and ask ourselves what this mission was really all about. And now that we've (sort of) arrived, what do we do now? This is when we stop and ask ourselves what's really important to us. *What really matters?*

Hopefully, what matters most is not so much where and how we live—but the ways our lives touch and interact with those around us. Hopefully, all these improvements to our lives and habitats were made so we could enjoy our time with people more. Because, when we get right down to it, that's what really matters. Isn't it?

CELEBRATING PEOPLE

1. *List some specific things you'd like to do with, and for, your closest loved ones.*
2. *Consider ways you can use and share your home to foster better relationships.*
3. *Plan a people event (big or small) that will be memorable to you and others.*
4. *Consider inviting someone you barely know for coffee or tea.*

PRAYER

Dear God, Thank You for where You have brought me.
But remind me of what really matters. Show me the people You
want me to touch with Your love. Amen

Teach Our Children Well

Train children in the right way, and when old,
they will not stray.

—Proverbs 22:6

Whether we have children of our own (in or out of the home) or other young friends and relatives, we, as adults on this earth, are all responsible for instructing the younger generation. And perhaps the best way to teach anyone is by example. So, hopefully, we've had some small sets of eyes watching us and learning from us simply by seeing our actions.

But there are other ways to teach. We can involve young ones in the actual doing, inviting them to participate in making their habitats a better place to live. And we can show them fun ways to be generous and give away the stuff they no longer need and use. And we can also encourage them to take some ecological responsibility for the world they live in. And hopefully, unlike us, they'll learn these lessons while they're young.

CLUTTER ATTACK

Children's toys and clothes quickly turn into clutter because they regularly outgrow them and because they continually acquire more of them. So consider planning a clutter attack before Christmas this year. Give junior a box for outgrown clothes (for the homeless) and a box for outgrown toys (for a favorite thrift shop). Do this again about six months later (or before a birthday).

PRAYER

Heavenly Father, help me to take responsibility for teaching (through my example) the young people around me. Show me how to help this next generation. Amen

A Grateful Heart

O Lord my God, I will give thanks to you forever.
—Psalm 30:12

And now as we approach the end of our clutter journey (at least in this little book, though hopefully not in real life!) perhaps it's time for us to take a moment to be truly thankful for where we've been, how we've changed, and where we're going. For learning becomes truly meaningful when we experience it with sincere gratitude. When we can look back and honestly (from the heart) express our thankfulness—then we have learned something!

So, let's remember to take some quiet time to reflect on what we've learned about ourselves, our lives, our homes. And let's ask ourselves if we're really glad we took the journey, or if we would have preferred to save ourselves the trouble and remain behind. Hopefully, we're glad for the experience. Hopefully, we can see where we've been and are grateful to be where we've come. And, hopefully, we're looking forward, even more, to where we are going!

A MOMENT OF THANKS

1. *Take time to thank God for leading you along.*
2. *Consider writing yourself a "thank you" note (in your journal).*
3. *Thank the people in your home who've patiently put up with some tough transitions.*

PRAYER

Dear God, thank You for all You've been doing in my life!
Teach me to have a truly grateful heart—in all things—and
show me ways to show my gratitude to others. Amen

Commitment to Continue

Finally, be strong in the Lord and in the strength of his power.
—Ephesians 6:10

It's hard to believe we've actually made it all the way through this little book together. It's as if we've become a circle of recovering clutterer friends! Maybe we'll even start that online clutterers' help group someday. But just because our book ends here doesn't mean that our journey will end. Because, as we all know, we must continue taking the things we've learned on with us, throughout our entire lives.

So maybe it's time we made a real promise to ourselves (and to God) that we will continue in our commitment against clutter, and that we're committed to strive for a better life, remaining free from the bondage of too much stuff. And as a result we (and our loved ones) will continue to enjoy our healthy and lovely clutter-free home.

MAKE A COMMITMENT

1. *Write down your commitment to yourself in your journal or plan book and date it.*
2. *Write down a similar commitment to God.*
3. *Ask God's blessing to help you honor these commitments.*

PRAYER

Almighty God, I commit my way to You.
But I need Your strength and help to keep this commitment.
Please, help me to come to You, every day of my life,
for encouragement and guidance. Amen

Notes

Notes

Notes

Notes

Notes

Notes

Notes

Notes

Notes

Notes

Notes

Notes

Notes

Notes

Notes

Notes

Notes

Notes